THE POWER OF SELF-MOTIVATION:

Unlocking Your Inner Drive

DR. AYNUL HASSAN

manda
Publishers

Title: The Power of Self-Motivation: Unlocking Your Inner Drive

Author: Dr. Aynul Hassan

First Published by Manda Publishers in 2025

ISBN: 978-93-6402-131-9
Price: 499/-
Manda Publishers
www.mandapublishers.com
publish@mandapublishers.com
+91 9999190496

Distributed by:
Amazon, Flipkart, Manda Publishers etc.

Printer:
Manipal Technologies

ACKNOWLEDGMENTS

This book would not have been possible without the love, patience, and encouragement of those closest to me.

To my family — thank you for being my foundation and my safe place. Your unwavering belief in me, even on the days I questioned myself, gave me the strength to keep writing. Every chapter carries a piece of your love, your laughter, and your quiet sacrifices. I am endlessly grateful for your support and understanding through the late nights and long silences.

To my friends, thank you for standing by me through this journey — for your words of encouragement, your thoughtful feedback, and your ability to lift my spirits when I needed it most. You reminded me that inspiration isn't found in isolation, but in connection, laughter, and shared moments.

This book is not just my achievement, but ours. Each of you has left an imprint on these pages, and I am deeply thankful to have you in my life

TABLE OF CONTENTS

CHAPTER 1: UNDERSTANDING SELF-MOTIVATION

INTRODUCTION TO SELF-MOTIVATION

Self-motivation is the internal drive that pushes you to act, accomplish goals, and maintain a sense of determination even when the going gets tough. It's the force that empowers you to start projects, keep working through obstacles, and finish what you set out to do without needing external rewards or encouragement.

In a world filled with distractions, external pressures, and societal expectations, self-motivation is the one resource that remains under your control. Whether you're trying to excel in your career, pursue a passion, get fit, or simply grow as a person, self-motivation acts as the fuel that keeps you moving toward your goals.

But what exactly is it? Is it something you're born with, or can it be developed?

Self-motivation is a learned skill. It's not just about pushing through laziness or waiting for inspiration to strike. It's about creating a mindset that fosters persistence, discipline, and a belief in your own abilities. It's the inner drive that propels you forward, even when there's no one else to cheer you on.

SELF-MOTIVATION VS. EXTERNAL MOTIVATION

Before diving deeper into the power of self-motivation, it's important to understand how it differs from external motivation.

- External Motivation comes from factors outside of you—such as rewards, praise, money, or the approval of others. While this type of motivation can be powerful in the short term, it often fades once the reward or recognition is removed. Think of it as a temporary boost that helps you take action but doesn't necessarily encourage sustained effort over time.
- Self-Motivation, on the other hand, comes from within. It's driven by your values, goals, desires, and sense of purpose. When you're self-motivated, you don't rely on external validation. Instead, your drive to achieve stems from your internal sense of accomplishment and satisfaction.

While external motivation can be a helpful push at times, self-motivation is the key to long-term success. It's not reliant on someone else's praise or recognition but rooted in your own ambitions and desires.

THE IMPORTANCE OF SELF-MOTIVATION

Self-motivation is not just about getting things done. It's about creating a mindset that empowers you to pursue your dreams, overcome setbacks, and maintain a sense of control over your life. It's essential for:

- Achieving Goals: Whether you're pursuing a professional goal, working on a personal project, or trying to develop a new skill, self-motivation is the key to getting from where you are to where you want to be.
- Building Resilience: Self-motivation helps you keep going even when things don't go as planned. It's what allows you to bounce back after failure and keep working toward success.
- Mastering Discipline: It's not just about motivation but also about creating the discipline to stay focused on your goals, even when the initial excitement fades. Self-motivation is what helps you build the habits that drive consistent progress.
- Sustaining Growth: With self-motivation, you remain in charge of your growth. It empowers you to continue learning, evolving, and developing without needing others to push you.

CAN SELF-MOTIVATION BE DEVELOPED?

The short answer: Yes. While some people may naturally have higher levels of motivation, it is a skill that anyone can cultivate. By developing an understanding of your inner drivers, setting clear goals, creating positive habits, and learning to maintain discipline, you can strengthen your ability to stay motivated—even in the face of challenges.

Self-motivation is the foundation for success, growth, and resilience. It gives you the strength to keep going when external motivation falters. Throughout this book, we will explore how to unlock the power of self-motivation and harness it to achieve the life you want—no matter what challenges lie ahead.

CHAPTER 2:
THE SCIENCE OF MOTIVATION

INTRODUCTION TO THE SCIENCE OF MOTIVATION

To truly understand how to harness self-motivation, it's essential to dive into the science behind it. Motivation isn't just an abstract concept or a feeling—it has a very real biological and psychological foundation. By understanding the science of motivation, you can start applying more effective strategies to stay motivated and achieve your goals.

Motivation is a complex process that involves our brain, emotions, and behaviors. From neurotransmitters to reward systems, understanding how motivation works at a biological level can give us insight into how to better manage our internal drive.

HOW MOTIVATION WORKS IN THE BRAIN

At its core, motivation is tied to the brain's reward systems. When we engage in actions that are pleasurable or beneficial, our brain releases dopamine, a neurotransmitter often referred to as the "feel-good" chemical. This creates a sense of pleasure or satisfaction that reinforces the behavior, making us want to do it again. This cycle is a key player in sustaining motivation.

- Dopamine and the Reward System: The brain's reward system is deeply linked to motivation. When you set a goal and achieve it—whether it's something big or small—your brain releases dopamine, giving you a sense of accomplishment. This chemical reward reinforces the behavior, which encourages you to take similar actions in the future.
- The "Pleasure-Pain" Balance: Motivation works through a balance of pleasure and pain. If we associate the task with pleasure (or positive outcomes), we are more likely to pursue it. Conversely, if we associate it with pain or discomfort, we may avoid it. Understanding this balance helps us reframe tasks that seem unpleasant, making them seem more appealing.

INTRINSIC VS. EXTRINSIC MOTIVATION

There are two main types of motivation: intrinsic and extrinsic. Both play crucial roles in how we engage with tasks and how long we remain motivated.

- Intrinsic Motivation: This comes from within. When we're intrinsically motivated, we perform a task because we find it inherently satisfying, fulfilling, or enjoyable. For example, pursuing a hobby or passion project out of love for the activity itself is an example of intrinsic motivation. This type of motivation is powerful because it's driven by internal values and interests, making it more sustainable over time.

- Extrinsic Motivation: This comes from external sources—rewards, recognition, or pressure from others. While extrinsic motivation can be effective in the short term, it is often not as lasting as intrinsic motivation. A promotion, salary increase, or award can certainly motivate someone to perform a task, but once that external reward is no longer present, motivation may dwindle.

In many cases, a combination of both intrinsic and extrinsic motivation is most effective, especially when we're working toward larger goals that require both passion and practical rewards.

THE ROLE OF HABITS AND ROUTINES

Habits are a powerful tool for sustaining motivation. Our brains love efficiency and routine, which is why creating positive habits can lead to long-term motivation and success. When you repeat a task often enough, it becomes a habit, and once something becomes a habit, it no longer requires as much mental effort or willpower to complete.

- The Habit Loop: The habit loop is a concept that refers to the three-step process that creates a habit:
    1. Cue: This is the trigger that prompts the behavior.
    2. Routine: The behavior or action itself.
    3. Reward: The positive outcome that reinforces the behavior.

By establishing routines that reward us with small wins, we create positive feedback loops that keep us motivated. For example, a workout routine becomes easier to maintain when we associate it with the positive feeling of accomplishment after a session.

THE "FLOW STATE" AND OPTIMAL MOTIVATION

Another important concept in the science of motivation is the flow state. Flow is a mental state where a person is fully immersed and engaged in an activity, experiencing deep focus and a sense of enjoyment. When in flow, time seems to disappear, and the activity feels almost effortless.

- Characteristics of Flow:
    1. Clear goals: Knowing exactly what you want to achieve.
    2. Immediate feedback: Knowing how well you are doing in real-time.
    3. Balance between challenge and skill: Tasks that challenge you just enough to keep you engaged but not overwhelm you.
    4. Complete immersion: You're fully present in the task, with no distractions.

Being able to enter the flow state regularly is a sign of intrinsic motivation at its peak. When you are in flow, you experience the perfect balance of challenge and competence, which propels you to continue performing at a high level.

THE IMPACT OF MOTIVATION ON PERFORMANCE

Motivation doesn't just affect whether or not we take action; it directly influences how well we perform. Studies have shown that individuals who are highly motivated tend to perform better, be more creative, and exhibit higher levels of persistence.

- Increased Focus and Productivity: When we're motivated, we focus more deeply on the task at hand. Motivation boosts our ability to filter out distractions, allowing us to be more productive.
- Higher Resilience and Creativity: Motivated individuals are more likely to bounce back from setbacks, adapt to changes, and persist in the face of challenges. Motivation fuels creativity by encouraging us to explore new ideas and solutions.
- Better Problem-Solving: Motivation enhances cognitive abilities, including critical thinking and problem-solving. When we're motivated, we're more likely to find innovative solutions to challenges, think outside the box, and tackle problems head-on.

THE MOTIVATION-EMOTION CONNECTION

Emotions and motivation are deeply intertwined. Positive emotions, such as excitement, pride, or satisfaction, often accompany motivation and drive us to keep going. On the other hand, negative emotions like frustration or fear of failure can diminish motivation and lead to procrastination or avoidance.

By managing our emotions—staying calm in the face of setbacks, celebrating small wins, and maintaining optimism—we can protect and nurture our motivation. Developing emotional resilience plays a key role in sustaining motivation in the long run.

CONCLUSION: HARNESSING THE SCIENCE OF MOTIVATION

Now that we have a clearer understanding of the science of motivation, we can begin applying this knowledge to increase our self-motivation. By recognizing the role of dopamine, the power of habits, and the importance of intrinsic rewards, we can set ourselves up for success.

The next step is to take this understanding and start applying it practically to your daily life—whether it's through setting meaningful goals, creating routines that support motivation, or fostering a mindset that welcomes challenge.

CHAPTER 3: OVERCOMING SELF-DOUBT AND NEGATIVE THOUGHTS

INTRODUCTION: THE STRUGGLE WITH SELF-DOUBT

Self-doubt is one of the most common barriers to self-motivation. It's that nagging voice in your head telling you that you're not good enough, that you'll fail, or that you're not capable of achieving your goals. While self-doubt is a normal part of being human, when left unchecked, it can hold you back from reaching your potential and even prevent you from taking action in the first place.

Negative thoughts can be overwhelming. They can make you question your abilities, undermine your confidence, and rob you of the energy needed to pursue your dreams. If you want to unlock your full potential and harness the power of self-motivation, overcoming self-doubt is crucial.

This chapter will explore the sources of self-doubt, how negative thoughts affect your motivation, and strategies to overcome these mental blocks and stay focused on your goals.

UNDERSTANDING THE ROOTS OF SELF-DOUBT

Self-doubt often stems from a variety of sources, including past experiences, fear of failure, and external influences. It can be triggered by perfectionism, comparison to others, or even the pressure to meet expectations. Let's break down some of the key causes:

1. Past Failures and Rejections: If you've faced failure or rejection in the past, you may carry that experience with you. These past setbacks can create a belief that you're destined to fail again, causing you to doubt your abilities and shy away from taking action.
2. Perfectionism: When you're constantly striving for perfection, the fear of not being "good enough" can paralyze you. The idea that you must do everything flawlessly before you even start often leads to procrastination and inaction.
3. Fear of Judgment: The fear of how others will perceive you can be a significant source of self-doubt. You may worry about criticism, rejection, or simply not living up to others' expectations.
4. Comparison to Others: In the age of social media, it's easy to compare yourself to others. Seeing someone else's success can trigger feelings of inadequacy, making you question your own progress or capabilities.
5. Negative Self-Talk: The inner dialogue we have with ourselves plays a huge role in self-doubt. If you

constantly tell yourself that you're not good enough or that you can't succeed, these negative thoughts become self-fulfilling prophecies.

HOW NEGATIVE THOUGHTS AFFECT MOTIVATION

Negative thoughts can be incredibly draining. When you're consumed by self-doubt, motivation takes a hit. Here's how negative thinking impacts your ability to stay motivated and productive:

1. Decreased Confidence: Self-doubt erodes your confidence, making it harder to take risks and put yourself out there. When you don't believe in your abilities, you're less likely to take action.
2. Fear of Failure: Negative thoughts about failure can prevent you from even trying. The fear of not succeeding may lead to procrastination, avoidance, or paralysis by analysis—essentially, overthinking without making any progress.
3. Mental Fatigue: Constantly battling negative thoughts can lead to mental exhaustion. When you're constantly questioning yourself, it consumes your energy and focus, leaving little room for productivity or positive action.
4. Self-Sabotage: Negative thinking often leads to self-sabotage. Whether it's through procrastination, perfectionism, or avoidance, these patterns of behavior keep you from moving forward toward your goals.
5. Lack of Resilience: Negative thoughts can hinder your ability to bounce back from setbacks. Instead of learning from failure and using it as a stepping stone, self-doubt may cause you to give up or become

discouraged.

STRATEGIES TO OVERCOME SELF-DOUBT AND NEGATIVE THOUGHTS

Overcoming self-doubt and negative thoughts is a gradual process that involves rewiring your mindset and developing healthier thought patterns. Here are some powerful strategies to help you conquer self-doubt and regain your motivation:

1. Challenge Negative Thoughts

The first step in overcoming self-doubt is to become aware of your negative thoughts. Once you recognize them, challenge their validity. Ask yourself:

- Is this thought based on facts or assumptions?
- Is there evidence to support this belief?
- What would I tell a friend who had the same thought?

Often, self-doubt stems from irrational beliefs or distorted thinking. By questioning these thoughts, you can begin to shift your mindset from negativity to a more balanced, realistic perspective.

2. Reframe Failure as a Learning Opportunity

One of the most common sources of self-doubt is the fear of failure. But failure is not the end—it's simply part of the learning process. Instead of viewing failure as something to fear, reframe it as a valuable opportunity for growth.

- Focus on the lessons learned: Every mistake or setback teaches you something new that brings you closer to success.

- Shift your perspective: Rather than thinking, "I failed," try thinking, "I'm one step closer to success because I learned something important."

When you embrace failure as part of the journey, you can remove the fear of it and keep moving forward.

3. Practice Self-Compassion

Many of us are our own harshest critics. But self-doubt often thrives in an environment of self-criticism. Practicing self-compassion—treating yourself with the same kindness, care, and understanding that you would offer to a friend—can help you overcome negativity.

- Acknowledge your feelings: Instead of ignoring or suppressing your doubts, recognize them without judgment. Understand that self-doubt is a normal part of being human.
- Offer yourself encouragement: Speak to yourself in a supportive and constructive way. Remind yourself of your strengths, past successes, and the hard work you've put in.

When your kind to yourself, you break the cycle of negativity and create space for growth and motivation.

4. Visualize Your Success

Visualization is a powerful tool for overcoming self-doubt. By imagining yourself succeeding, you can shift your focus away from fear and build confidence in your abilities.

- Create a clear mental picture: Visualize yourself reaching your goals, feeling proud, and enjoying the

rewards of your hard work.
- Engage all your senses: Try to make the visualization as vivid as possible. How does it feel, look, sound, or even smell when you succeed?

By regularly practicing visualization, you strengthen your belief in your abilities and create a mindset that supports your success.

5. Break Down Goals into Smaller, Achievable Steps

Self-doubt often emerges when a goal feels too overwhelming or unattainable. To combat this, break your goals into smaller, more manageable steps. This will make your objectives feel more achievable and will help you build momentum as you accomplish each step.

- Focus on progress, not perfection: Celebrate small wins along the way and use them as motivation to keep going.
- Set realistic expectations: Acknowledge that big goals take time, and it's okay to take small steps toward achieving them.

Each small victory will reinforce your confidence and reduce feelings of self-doubt.

6. Surround Yourself with Supportive People

The people around you can significantly influence your mindset. Surround yourself with individuals who uplift you, believe in your potential, and encourage your growth.

- Seek out mentors: Find someone who has experience and success in areas you're pursuing. Their guidance and support can help you navigate challenges and overcome doubts.
- Avoid negativity: Limit time spent with people who reinforce your insecurities or make you feel inadequate.

Support from others can provide the encouragement you need to overcome self-doubt and keep moving forward.

CONCLUSION: EMBRACING CONFIDENCE AND MOTIVATION

Overcoming self-doubt and negative thoughts is not an overnight process, but with practice, it's absolutely achievable. By challenging your negative beliefs, reframing failure, practicing self-compassion, visualizing success, and breaking down your goals, you can build the confidence and motivation needed to take action.

Remember, self-doubt is not a reflection of your true capabilities—it's simply a barrier that can be overcome with the right mindset. By taking control of your thoughts and beliefs, you can tap into your inner strength and unlock the motivation to pursue your goals with determination and confidence.

CHAPTER 4:

SETTING CLEAR AND ACHIEVABLE GOALS

INTRODUCTION: THE POWER OF GOAL-SETTING

One of the most powerful ways to ignite and sustain self-motivation is through goal-setting. Goals provide direction, purpose, and a roadmap for your actions. Without clear goals, it's easy to drift aimlessly, unsure of what you're working toward or why you're doing it. When you set clear, achievable goals, however, you create a sense of focus, commitment, and momentum that drives you forward—even when the going gets tough.

But not all goals are created equal. To truly unlock the power of goal-setting, you need to ensure that your goals are both clear and attainable. In this chapter, we will explore the importance of setting effective goals and provide you with a proven framework to make sure your goals are inspiring, actionable, and motivating.

WHY SETTING GOALS MATTERS

Goals are not just wishful thinking—they are the key to turning your dreams into reality. Setting clear goals helps you:

1. Provide Direction: Without goals, it's easy to feel lost or overwhelmed by life's distractions. Goals give you a clear path to follow, allowing you to direct your efforts toward what truly matters.

2. Increase Motivation: When you set a goal, especially one that excites you, it gives you something to work toward. The anticipation of reaching that goal fuels your motivation to take consistent action

3. Measure Progress: Goals provide a tangible way to track your progress. By breaking larger goals into smaller milestones, you can see how far you've come, which helps maintain motivation and build confidence.

4. Create a Sense of Purpose: Goals help you stay focused on what's important to you, creating a deeper sense of purpose and satisfaction. When you know why you're doing something, it becomes much easier to stay motivated.

5. Boost Confidence: Achieving your goals, even the small ones, builds your self-belief. Each success

reinforces your confidence and shows you that you have the ability to reach even greater heights.

THE SMART GOAL FRAMEWORK

One of the most widely used and effective methods for setting clear and achievable goals is the SMART framework. This framework helps you clarify your goals, making them more actionable and measurable. Here's a breakdown of the SMART criteria:

1. Specific: Your goal should be clear and unambiguous. A specific goal is focused and answers the questions: What do I want to accomplish? Why is this goal important? Who is involved? Where will it take place?

Example: Instead of saying "I want to get fit," say "I want to run a 5k race in three months."

2. Measurable: It's important to quantify your goal so that you can track progress. Ask yourself: How will I know when I've achieved my goal? What metrics or criteria can I use to measure success?

Example: "I want to run 3 miles every week until the race."

3. Achievable: Your goal should be realistic and attainable, considering your current resources, skills, and time. Setting an achievable goal ensures that you challenge yourself, but without setting yourself up for failure. Ask yourself: Do I have the necessary resources to achieve this goal? Is this goal possible within the time frame?

Example: "I'll start by running two times a week, gradually increasing to three times a week as I build my stamina."

4. Relevant: Your goal should align with your broader

life aspirations, values, and long-term objectives. A relevant goal matters to you and fits into your bigger picture. Ask yourself: Why is this goal important to me? How does it align with my values or long-term goals?

Example: "Running a 5k will improve my fitness and health, which is important to me for maintaining a healthy lifestyle."

5. Time-bound: Every goal needs a deadline or time frame. Without a clear time frame, there's no sense of urgency, and your motivation may fizzle out. Ask yourself: When do I want to achieve this goal? What is the time frame for success?

Example: "I will run the 5k race on [specific date], and I will train for three months leading up to that."

By setting SMART goals, you create a clear path toward success that is both motivating and achievable.

BREAKING DOWN BIG GOALS INTO SMALLER STEPS

Large, long-term goals can often feel overwhelming. But when you break them down into smaller, manageable steps, they become much more achievable. Here's how to approach breaking down big goals:

1. Identify the Big Picture Goal

Start with your larger, long-term goal. This is the "what" you want to accomplish.

Example: "I want to write a book."

2. Break It Into Smaller, Actionable Milestones

Once you've identified your big picture goal, break it down into smaller milestones. These should be smaller, achievable goals that act as stepping stones toward your ultimate goal.

Example:

- Research topic and outline book (1 month)
- Write first draft of book (3 months)
- Edit and revise manuscript (2 months)

3. Set Micro-Goals for Each Milestone

Next, break each milestone into even smaller, more actionable steps—these are your micro-goals. Micro-goals are bite-sized actions that you can take on a daily or weekly basis.

Example (for writing a book):

- Write 500 words every morning for the next 30 days.
- Research 3 articles every week.
- Edit one chapter per week.

4. Establish Deadlines for Each Micro-Goal

Setting deadlines for each micro-goal ensures you stay on track and keeps you accountable. Use your calendar to plan when you will complete each task.

Example: "I'll finish writing 500 words per day for the next 30 days, and I'll aim to have the first draft finished by the end of the month."

Breaking down your goals in this way reduces the feeling of being overwhelmed and provides a clear roadmap for action.

STAYING FLEXIBLE: ADJUSTING YOUR GOALS WHEN NECESSARY

While it's important to set clear and actionable goals, life doesn't always go according to plan. Sometimes, obstacles arise, circumstances change, or you may realize that your original goal needs to be adjusted. And that's okay.

Here are a few tips for staying flexible while still achieving success:

1. Reevaluate Goals Regularly: Check in on your progress periodically. If you're not making the progress you'd hoped for, or if something in your life changes, adjust your goals accordingly.

2. Be Kind to Yourself: It's normal for things not to always go according to plan. Instead of beating yourself up, learn from the experience and adjust your approach.

3. Celebrate Progress, Not Just Results: Even if you haven't reached your ultimate goal yet, take time to celebrate the milestones and progress you've made along the way.

4. Stay Open to New Opportunities: Sometimes the path to your goal may look different than you expected. Be open to new ways of reaching your destination.

VISUALIZING SUCCESS: KEEP YOUR EYES ON THE PRIZE

Visualization is a powerful tool to keep you motivated and focused on your goals. By vividly imagining the end result of your goal, you activate your brain's reward system and boost your sense of motivation.

- Visualize the outcome: Picture yourself achieving your goal and savor the positive feelings that come with success.
- Focus on the process: Also visualize the steps you need to take to reach your goal. This reinforces your commitment to the journey.

CONCLUSION: GOAL SETTING AS A TOOL FOR MOTIVATION

Setting clear and achievable goals is one of the most effective ways to sustain your motivation. When you have a clear vision of what you want to achieve and a well-structured plan to get there, you're much more likely to stay focused, energized, and driven.

Use the SMART framework to create goals that are specific, measurable, achievable, relevant, and time-bound. Break your larger goals into smaller steps, and adjust them as needed to stay on track. By doing so, you'll be able to maintain momentum and keep moving toward success, one step at a time.

PRACTICAL EXERCISES FOR SETTING CLEAR AND ACHIEVABLE GOALS

In this section, we'll provide a set of practical exercises and tools that will help you apply the principles of goal setting and tracking progress to your own life. These exercises are designed to help you clarify your goals, break them down into manageable steps, and track your progress along the way.

1. Goal-Setting Worksheet

The goal-setting worksheet will guide you through the process of creating clear, achievable goals using the SMART framework. Follow the prompts below to develop your personal goals.

GOAL-SETTING WORKSHEET

- Goal Name: What is the specific goal you want to achieve?

  (Example: Run a 5k race, Write a book, Start a side business, etc.)

- Why is this goal important to you? (Reflect on the deeper motivation behind the goal. What is the driving force that makes this goal meaningful for you?)

- **SMART Breakdown:**

  - Specific: What exactly do you want to accomplish? Be precise.

    (Example: I want to run a 5k race.)

  - Measurable: How will you measure progress or success? What metrics will you use?

    (Example: I will track my running distance each week.)

  - Achievable: Is this goal realistic and possible for you to achieve within your timeframe? What resources or skills do you need?

(Example: I can train 3 times a week and gradually increase my running distance.)

- Relevant: Why is this goal worth pursuing right now? How does it align with your long-term vision?

  (Example: Running a 5k will improve my fitness and health, which is important for my overall well-being.)

- Time-Bound: What is the deadline for this goal? When do you plan to achieve it?

  (Example: I will run the 5k race in 3 months.)

- Break It Down into Milestones: Identify smaller milestones that you can celebrate along the way.

  (Example: Complete a 1-mile run by week 1, complete a 3-mile run by week 6.)

- Action Plan: List the specific actions you will take each week to achieve your goal.

  (Example: Week 1: Run 1 mile every Tuesday and Thursday. Week 2: Run 2 miles every Tuesday and Thursday, etc.)

2. Daily/Weekly Goal Tracker

Tracking your progress is essential for staying motivated and accountable. This goal tracker will help you monitor your actions and see how close you are to achieving your goals.

How to Use the Tracker:

- At the beginning of each week, write down your goals and action steps.
- At the end of each day, review whether you've accomplished what you set out to do.
- Reflect on your progress weekly, and adjust your plan if necessary.

Goal Tracker (Daily/Weekly)

Date	Goal	Action Steps	Progress Made	Notes/Reflections
Week 1, Day 1	Run 1 mile	Run 1 mile on the treadmill	Completed 1 mile	Felt great, will aim for better pace next time.
Week 1, Day 2	Run 1 mile	Run 1 mile outside	Ran 1 mile in 10 minutes	Felt challenged but pushed through.
Week 1, Day 3	Write 500 words	Write a daily 500-word draft	Wrote 500 words	Words flowed easily today, great progress!
...	...	...	...	...

- Progress Made: Track how much you've accomplished for each action step.
- Notes/Reflections: Write down any thoughts, challenges, or positive experiences you've had. This helps you adjust your actions for the next day.

3. Weekly Reflection

Taking the time to reflect on your progress each week can keep you motivated and ensure that you're staying on track. This exercise helps you identify both successes and areas that need improvement.

How to Use the Reflection Exercise: At the end of each week, take a moment to reflect on your progress. Ask yourself the following questions:

Weekly Reflection

- What progress did I make this week toward my goal? (Example: I ran 2 miles consistently, wrote 3 new chapters of my book.)
- What challenges or obstacles did I face this week? (Example: I struggled to stay motivated to run on cold mornings.)
- What worked well for me this week? (Example: I managed to stick to my schedule and was able to push through difficult moments.)
- What can I improve next week? (Example: I'll set out my running clothes the night before to avoid the morning cold.)
- Am I still on track to meet my goal by the deadline? (Example: Yes, I'm consistently increasing my distance and am on target to run the full 5k in three months.)
- How can I stay motivated in the coming week? (Example: I'll celebrate each small victory, like completing a 2-mile run, and remind myself why I'm doing this.)

4. Accountability Partner or Mentor Check-In

Sometimes, sharing your goals with someone else can provide the extra push you need. An accountability partner or mentor can hold you accountable, provide encouragement, and help you stay motivated.

How to Use the Accountability Partner Check-In:

- Share your goals and action steps with your accountability partner.
- Set a weekly or bi-weekly check-in time to update them on your progress.
- Be open to feedback and support.

Accountability Check-In Questions

1. What goals did I set for this week?
2. Did I achieve the goals I set for this week?
3. What challenges did I face, and how did I overcome them?
4. What is my plan for the coming week to stay on track?

5. Visualizing Your Success

Visualization can significantly enhance your motivation and keep you focused on your goals. To practice visualization, take a few moments each day to imagine yourself successfully achieving your goal.

Visualization Exercise:

- Find a quiet place and close your eyes.
- Picture yourself having already achieved your goal.

Visualize the emotions, the sense of accomplishment, and the rewards.

- Engage all your senses in the visualization. What does success look like? What does it feel like? What are you hearing or experiencing?
- Spend at least 5–10 minutes visualizing your success every day to reinforce your motivation.

CONCLUSION: STAYING ON TRACK

By using these exercises and tools, you can break down your goals into manageable steps, track your progress, and stay focused on your path to success. Remember that the key to achieving your goals is consistency. Keep showing up, reflect on your progress, and adjust as needed. Celebrate your small wins along the way, and before you know it, you'll have achieved the goals you set for yourself.

CHAPTER 5: BUILDING MOMENTUM AND STAYING CONSISTENT

INTRODUCTION: THE POWER OF CONSISTENCY

When it comes to achieving any goal, the ability to build momentum and stay consistent is often what separates those who succeed from those who fall short. Motivation can be fleeting, but consistency is what keeps you moving forward, even on the days when you don't feel like it.

Momentum is like a snowball. At first, the effort needed to get started is significant, but as you build momentum and stay consistent, progress becomes easier, faster, and more rewarding. In this chapter, we will explore how to build that momentum, the importance of consistency, and how to overcome the challenges that may cause you to lose focus.

THE SCIENCE OF MOMENTUM: HOW SMALL ACTIONS ADD UP

Momentum is a powerful force, and the process of building it is often a matter of taking small, deliberate actions over time. Here's how momentum works:

1. Start Small: At the beginning of any new project or goal, it's crucial to start with manageable, small steps. These small actions don't feel overwhelming, and as you continue, the success of completing these smaller tasks gives you confidence and builds momentum.
2. Build on Success: As you accomplish small tasks, you create a sense of progress. This sense of accomplishment provides a psychological boost, which fuels your desire to take on the next task. It's a positive feedback loop: the more success you experience, the more momentum you build, and the easier it becomes to keep going.
3. Compound Progress: Just like compound interest in finance, small, consistent actions taken over time lead to exponential results. What might seem like insignificant progress at first quickly adds up. The key is staying committed to the process.
4. Energy from Action: Often, people wait to feel motivated before they take action. However, motivation often follows action, not the other way around. The simple act of starting—whether it's writing a paragraph, completing a 10-minute workout, or setting up a meeting—can spark motivation and keep you going.

CREATING MOMENTUM: PRACTICAL STRATEGIES

Now that we understand the science behind momentum, let's explore some practical strategies to build and maintain it in your daily life:

1. Start with Daily Habits

The best way to build momentum is through consistent, daily habits. These habits don't need to be huge or time-consuming; in fact, smaller, easier-to-commit-to actions are more sustainable over time. The goal is to do something each day that brings you closer to your larger goal.

- Example: If your goal is to write a book, set aside 30 minutes every day to write. Even if you don't feel like writing, simply sitting down and committing to the time will help you build momentum.
- Tip: Use the "Two-Minute Rule" to get started. Commit to working on your goal for just two minutes. Often, once you start, it's easier to keep going.

2. Track Your Progress Regularly

One of the most powerful ways to stay consistent is by visually tracking your progress. Tracking helps you see how far you've come and reminds you of your successes, which fuels your motivation to continue.

- Example: If you're working toward a fitness goal, mark each workout on a calendar or use an app to log your activity. Seeing a streak of successful workouts motivates you to keep it going.
- Tip: Use habit-tracking apps, journals, or charts to monitor your daily or weekly progress. Visual progress is motivating and reinforces the idea that you're moving forward.

3. Create Routines and Schedules

Creating a daily or weekly routine ensures that consistency becomes part of your lifestyle. By allocating specific times for specific tasks, you eliminate the decision-making process that can slow you down.

- Example: If you're building a business, set aside an hour each morning to work on your business plan or outreach strategy. Having a set time makes it easier to stick with it.
- Tip: Schedule your most important tasks at times when you're most energetic or focused, such as first thing in the morning or after a break.

OVERCOMING CHALLENGES AND STAYING CONSISTENT

Staying consistent isn't always easy. There will be days when you feel exhausted, uninspired, or discouraged. Life can throw curveballs that disrupt your routines. Here are some strategies to help you stay consistent, even when faced with obstacles:

1. Embrace Imperfection

Perfectionism can often hinder consistency. If you expect yourself to do everything perfectly every time, you may find yourself paralyzed by fear of failure. The key to building momentum is embracing imperfection and allowing yourself to take action, even if it's not perfect.

- Tip: Remind yourself that "done is better than perfect." Each action, even if it's small or imperfect, gets you closer to your goal.

2. Break Down Big Goals into Smaller Tasks

Large goals can feel overwhelming, and the more overwhelmed you feel, the more likely you are to procrastinate or give up. Breaking down big goals into smaller, more manageable tasks reduces the stress and makes it easier to stay consistent.

- Example: If you're writing a book, break the task down into smaller steps, like outlining chapters, writing 500 words a day, or editing a section at a time.
- Tip: Focus on one small task at a time and celebrate each accomplishment. The key is to keep moving forward, no matter how small the steps.

3. Set Reminders and Triggers

One of the easiest ways to ensure you stay consistent is by setting reminders or creating environmental triggers that prompt you to take action.

- Example: Set daily reminders on your phone to remind you to write, exercise, or work on your goal.
- Tip: Link a new habit to an existing one. For example, if your goal is to read more, make it a habit to read for 10 minutes after your morning coffee.

4. Stay Accountable to Yourself and Others

Having an accountability system can greatly improve your chances of staying consistent. This could be a friend, mentor, or an online community that keeps you on track and motivated.

- Tip: Share your goals with someone you trust and schedule regular check-ins to discuss your progress.

Knowing that someone is expecting you to follow through can be a powerful motivator.

MAINTAINING MOMENTUM: KEEP THE FIRE BURNING

Building momentum is just the beginning. Once you've gained momentum, it's important to keep that fire burning. Here are a few ways to ensure you keep going once you've started:

1. Celebrate Your Wins

Every small success matters. Celebrating milestones, whether big or small, is essential for maintaining motivation. It reminds you of how far you've come and reinforces the positive habit you're building.

- Example: After hitting a weekly goal, reward yourself with a small treat or break. If you've worked out consistently for a month, treat yourself to a new workout outfit or a relaxing activity.

2. Reassess Your Goals Regularly

While consistency is key, it's important to reassess your goals periodically. This helps you make sure that you're still on the right track and allows you to adjust if necessary. Sometimes, goals or strategies need to evolve as you grow.

- Tip: Set aside time each month or quarter to evaluate your progress, reflect on what's working, and tweak your approach as needed.

3. Stay Inspired and Energized

Even the most consistent individuals experience moments of burnout or lack of motivation. When this happens, it's important to find ways to reignite your passion and energy.

- Tip: Surround yourself with sources of inspiration—books, podcasts, motivational speakers, or peers who are also working toward similar goals. This keeps your energy levels high and reinforces your commitment to your goals.

CONCLUSION: THE SECRET TO LONG-TERM SUCCESS

Building momentum and staying consistent is the cornerstone of achieving your goals. While motivation may fluctuate, consistency will always keep you moving forward. By starting small, tracking your progress, building supportive habits, and staying flexible in the face of challenges, you'll be able to keep the momentum alive and push through even the most difficult times.

Remember: Momentum doesn't happen overnight. It's a result of continuous, small actions that, over time, lead to extraordinary outcomes. Stay consistent, keep building on your successes, and watch how your momentum propels you toward your ultimate goals.

Practical Exercises for Building Momentum and Staying Consistent

In this section, we'll provide exercises to help you put the strategies discussed in the chapter into practice. These exercises will guide you in building momentum, staying consistent, and maintaining long-term motivation as you work toward your goals.

1. Consistency Checklist

The Consistency Checklist is a simple tool to help you stay on track and hold yourself accountable. This checklist ensures that you're consistently taking action toward your goal, even if it's in small steps.

How to Use the Consistency Checklist:

- Step 1: Each day, list the actions you need to take to make progress toward your goal.
- Step 2: At the end of the day, check off each action you completed.
- Step 3: Reflect on your progress and note any challenges you faced.
- Step 4: Review your checklist at the end of each week to evaluate your consistency and progress.

Consistency Checklist

Date	Goal	Action Steps for the Day	Completed?	Notes/Challenges
Monday	Write a book	Write 500 words	✓	Felt inspired, completed 550 words today!
Tuesday	Write a book	Write 500 words	✗	Struggled to focus, will try again tomorrow
Wednesday	Exercise (Run 3 miles)	Run 3 miles	✓	Felt good after the run, great energy boost!
Thursday	Exercise (Run 3	Run 3 miles	✓	Speed improved, felt stronger!

	miles)			
Friday	Write a book	Write 500 words	✓	A little challenging, but finished!

Accountability is one of the most powerful tools for staying consistent. By tracking your progress and regularly checking in on your goals, you create an additional layer of commitment. Use this tracking sheet to check in with yourself weekly and assess your accountability.

How to Use the Accountability Tracking Sheet:

- Step 1: At the start of each week, list your goals and the actions required to achieve them.
- Step 2: At the end of the week, assess your progress and reflect on any obstacles or successes you encountered.
- Step 3: If possible, check in with an accountability partner to discuss your progress and goals.

Weekly Accountability Tracking Sheet

Week of	Goal(s) for the Week	Action Steps for the Week	Progress Made	Challenges Faced	Next Week's Plan
Week 1	Write a book (5,000 words)	Write 500 words per day	Completed 3,000 words	Had trouble focusing on Monday	Focus on writing first thing in the morning
Wee	Exercise	Run 3	Ran 2.5	Struggled	Plan run

k 2	(Run 5k)	miles on Monday, Wednesday, and Friday	miles on Mon & Wed	with time management	earlier in the day
Week 3	Learn a new skill (Spanish)	Complete 30 minutes of Duolingo each day	Completed 5 out of 7 days	Missed Thursday, but caught up Friday	Set reminder on phone to do daily lessons
Week 4	Start a side business	Research business idea, create a business plan	Finished research	Felt overwhelmed with information	Break tasks into smaller chunks

3. Momentum-Building Habit Tracker

Use this tool to track the consistency of your habits that contribute to your long-term success. The more consistent you are, the stronger your momentum will be. This tracker will help you stay accountable to daily actions that gradually move you toward your goal.

How to Use the Momentum-Building Habit Tracker:

- Step 1: Identify the habits or actions that will help you achieve your goal.
- Step 2: Each day, mark off whether you performed the habit.
- Step 3: At the end of the week, assess your consistency and reflect on how building small actions helped you gain momentum.

Momentum-Building Habit Tracker

Wee k of	Habit/A ction	M on	T ue	W ed	T hu	F ri	S at	Su n	To tal	Notes
Mar ch 1-7	Write 500 words daily	✓	✓	✓	✓	✓	✗	✓	6/7	Feelin g strong, but missed Sat
Mar ch 8-14	Run 3 miles 3x a week	✓	✗	✓	✓				3/3	Great week, full streak!
Mar ch 1-7	Study Spanish 30 mins daily	✓	✓	✓	✓	✓	✓	✓	7/7	Routin e is becom ing autom atic!

4. Daily Action Prompt

Sometimes, we need a little extra push to start taking action. The following prompt will help you set the intention for your day and ensure that you take at least one small step toward your goal, no matter what.

How to Use the Daily Action Prompt:

- Step 1: Each morning or the night before, write down one action you will take today that will bring you closer to your goal. Keep it simple, concrete, and achievable.
- Step 2: At the end of the day, reflect on your progress and whether you were able to take the action you planned.

Daily Action Prompt

Date	Action for the Day	Progress Made	Reflection
March 1	Write 500 words	Wrote 500 words	Felt motivated after getting started.
March 2	Run 3 miles	Ran 3 miles	Struggled at first, but felt great afterward.
March 3	Spend 30 minutes learning Spanish	Completed 30 minutes of Duolingo	Felt proud of the consistency!
March 4	Plan out business structure	Wrote out 3 main business goals	Need to refine next steps, but progress made.
March 5	Read 1 chapter of a book about goal-setting	Finished chapter 1 of the book	Inspired to take more consistent action!

5. Reflection and Adjustment Exercise

At the end of each week, take a moment to reflect on your progress and adjust your strategy as needed. Use these prompts to evaluate how consistent you've been and identify any obstacles that need to be addressed.

How to Use the Reflection and Adjustment Exercise:

- Step 1: Reflect on the past week and assess your consistency and momentum.
- Step 2: Identify any obstacles or challenges that prevented you from staying on track.
- Step 3: Adjust your action plan for the coming week based on what you learned.

Reflection and Adjustment Exercise

- What were my biggest wins this week? (Example: I wrote 3,000 words and ran a total of 9 miles.)
- What challenges or obstacles did I face? (Example: I felt tired and skipped a couple of workouts.)
- What could I have done differently to stay more consistent?
  (Example: I could have planned my workouts earlier in the day to avoid distractions.)
- How can I adjust my action plan for next week? (Example: I will set out my running clothes the night before and set an alarm to remind myself to write at 8 a.m.)

CONCLUSION: KEEPING THE MOMENTUM ALIVE

By using these tools, you'll be able to track your progress, stay accountable, and reflect on your journey toward your goals. Consistency doesn't happen overnight, but with the right mindset, accountability, and small daily actions, you will build momentum that propels you toward success.

Additional Tools for Building Momentum and Staying Consistent

In addition to the exercises and tools already provided, here are a few more strategies and tools you can use to further enhance your momentum and consistency. These will help you stay on track, especially during challenging periods when motivation may dip.

6. The "5-Minute Rule" for Overcoming Procrastination

The "5-Minute Rule" is a powerful strategy for overcoming procrastination and pushing through resistance. Often, the hardest part of any task is simply getting started. The idea behind this rule is simple: commit to working on a task for just five minutes.

How to Use the 5-Minute Rule:

- Step 1: When you feel resistance or procrastination, commit to working on your task for just 5 minutes.
- Step 2: Often, the hardest part is getting started. Once you've worked for 5 minutes, you may find that you want to continue because the task feels less daunting.
- Step 3: Even if you only do 5 minutes, you've still made progress, and you've kept your momentum going

Example: If you're writing a book and feel stuck, tell yourself you'll write for just 5 minutes. You may end up writing for much longer once you've broken the initial barrier.

7. The "Why" Exercise: Reconnecting with Your Purpose

One of the most powerful ways to stay motivated during challenging periods is to reconnect with the why behind your goal. When motivation is low, remembering your deep, personal reasons for pursuing a goal can reignite your drive.

How to Use the "Why" Exercise:

- Step 1: Write down your goal in one sentence.
- Step 2: Ask yourself, "Why is this goal important to

me?" and write down your answer.
- Step 3: Keep asking "Why?" until you can identify a core reason or emotion behind your goal. You may find that your goal is tied to a deeper sense of purpose, such as personal growth, the desire to help others, or creating a better future for yourself or your family.

Example: If your goal is to start a business, your deeper "why" might be, "I want to create a business that allows me to have financial freedom and spend more time with my family." Reconnecting with this deeper motivation can help you push through tough moments.

8. The Accountability Partner Check-In

Sometimes, all you need to stay on track is an accountability partner—someone who you check in with regularly about your progress. Knowing that someone else is counting on you to stay consistent can be a powerful motivator, especially during tough times.

How to Use the Accountability Partner Check-In:

- Step 1: Find an accountability partner who shares similar goals or someone who supports your personal growth.
- Step 2: Set up regular check-ins with them (daily, weekly, or bi-weekly) to report on your progress.
- Step 3: During each check-in, discuss your successes, challenges, and next steps.
- Step 4: If possible, set small rewards or consequences based on whether you met your goals.

Example: You might have a weekly check-in with your accountability partner where you both discuss how many pages you've written in your book or how many workouts you've completed. Sharing successes and challenges with someone else can increase your commitment and reduce feelings of isolation during tough times.

9. The "Celebrate Small Wins" Technique

Celebrating small wins is crucial for maintaining momentum. Celebrations, no matter how small, create positive reinforcement and remind you that you're progressing.

How to Celebrate Small Wins:

- Step 1: Each time you complete a milestone or reach a small goal, take a moment to celebrate it.
- Step 2: Your celebration can be anything that feels rewarding—whether it's taking a break, enjoying a treat, or doing something you love.
- Step 3: Recognize that each small step is part of the bigger journey. Celebrating these milestones helps to prevent burnout and keep your morale high.

Example: After hitting a goal of writing 1,000 words, reward yourself by watching an episode of your favorite show or taking a walk. These small rewards will reinforce the habit of taking consistent action.

10. Visualization for Motivation

Visualization is a powerful technique for staying motivated, especially when facing challenges. By vividly imagining the successful completion of your goal, you can harness the emotional power of that vision to fuel your drive.

How to Use Visualization for Motivation:

- Step 1: Take a quiet moment to close your eyes and visualize yourself achieving your goal. Use all five senses—imagine what you will see, hear, and feel when you accomplish it.
- Step 2: Focus on the positive emotions that come with success: the pride, the excitement, the sense of fulfillment.
- Step 3: Visualize how your life will be different after achieving your goal. What will change? How will you feel? Hold onto that vision whenever you face setbacks.

Example: If your goal is to run a marathon, visualize crossing the finish line, feeling the sense of accomplishment, and celebrating with friends and family. This powerful mental image will remind you why the hard work is worth it.

11. The Pomodoro Technique: Managing Energy, Not Just Time

Staying consistent requires energy, and sometimes the challenge isn't about willpower but about managing your energy levels. The Pomodoro Technique is a time-management strategy that helps you stay focused without burning out by working in short bursts.

How to Use the Pomodoro Technique:

- Step 1: Choose a task you want to focus on.

- Step 2: Set a timer for 25 minutes (one "Pomodoro") and work with full concentration.
- Step 3: After 25 minutes, take a 5-minute break to recharge.
- Step 4: After completing four Pomodoros, take a longer break (15-30 minutes).
- Step 5: Repeat the process, ensuring that you're balancing work and rest.

Example: If you're writing your book and feeling overwhelmed, break the task into 25-minute writing sessions with 5-minute breaks. By focusing intensely for a short time and then taking a break, you can maintain high productivity without getting mentally exhausted.

STAYING MOTIVATED DURING CHALLENGING PERIODS

Even with the best systems in place, there will be times when motivation wanes, or life throws challenges your way. During these tough moments, it's important to lean into strategies that will help you stay resilient and focused. Here are a few additional ideas for staying motivated when you face setbacks:

1. Remember Your "Why": Whenever you feel discouraged, remind yourself of why you set this goal in the first place. Reconnect with your deep motivations, and use that to reignite your determination.
2. Break Things Down: When tasks seem overwhelming, break them down into smaller, more manageable pieces. Focus on the next small step, and don't worry about everything at once.

3. Practice Self-Compassion: Be kind to yourself. It's easy to get frustrated with yourself during challenging times, but self-criticism only adds to stress. Instead, practice self-compassion and recognize that setbacks are part of the journey.
4. Find Inspiration: When motivation is low, find a source of inspiration. Read about others who have overcome similar challenges, listen to motivational podcasts, or seek out a mentor or peer who can offer encouragement.
5. Reevaluate Your Approach: If you're stuck or facing constant roadblocks, it may be a sign that you need to reevaluate your approach. Are there better methods or systems you can try? Adjusting your strategy may breathe new life into your goals.

CONCLUSION: KEEP GOING, EVEN WHEN IT'S HARD

Staying consistent and motivated over the long term is a challenge, but with the right tools and mindset, you can build momentum that will carry you through tough times. The key is to stay focused on your "why," track your progress, celebrate your small wins, and adjust your strategies when necessary. Every small action you take adds up over time, bringing you one step closer to your ultimate goal.

Guidance on Overcoming Specific Challenges and Motivational Strategies for Setbacks

Even with the best intentions, setbacks are inevitable. Whether it's a lack of time, unexpected obstacles, or a dip in motivation, knowing how to handle these challenges can be the key to achieving long-term success. Below are strategies that will help you stay motivated and push through common setbacks.

1. Lack of Time: How to Stay Consistent When You're Busy

One of the most common challenges is feeling like there's not enough time to work on your goals. Whether you're balancing work, family, or other responsibilities, time constraints can leave you feeling stuck.

Strategies to Stay Consistent:

- Prioritize Your Goals: Make sure that the actions you're taking align with your most important goals. If your time is limited, you need to be intentional about what you work on. Focus on high-impact activities that get you closer to your goal.
- Time Blocking: Block off specific times in your schedule for goal-related tasks. Even 20-30 minutes of focused work can add up. Use a calendar or planner to schedule your time in advance and treat these time slots as non-negotiable.
- Micro-Tasks: Break down larger tasks into smaller, more manageable parts. When time is tight, commit to doing just one small task, such as writing 100 words, completing one workout set, or reading a chapter. It's better to make small progress than to wait for the "perfect time."
- Combine Tasks: If possible, combine your goal-related activities with other tasks. For example, listen to a podcast about your area of interest while commuting, or do light stretching exercises while watching TV. This way, you're multitasking and staying productive.

2. Overwhelm and Stress: Staying Motivated When You Feel Like Giving Up

It's easy to get overwhelmed, especially when you're working toward big goals or when life throws multiple challenges your way. The feeling of burnout or stress can be paralyzing, making it hard to stay consistent.

Strategies to Combat Overwhelm:

- Take Small Steps: Overwhelm often comes from trying to do too much at once. Break your tasks down into bite-sized pieces, and focus on taking the next small step. Completing smaller, manageable tasks will build your confidence and reduce feelings of overwhelm.
- Practice Mindfulness or Meditation: Stress and anxiety can cloud your motivation. Try mindfulness exercises, deep breathing, or meditation to help reduce stress and refocus your mind. Even just a few minutes of quiet reflection can help you regain clarity and energy.
- Take a Break: If you're feeling burnt out, it might be a sign that you need to step away for a while. Taking a short break or even a day off can help you recharge and come back to your work with renewed focus and energy.
- Focus on What You Can Control: When life feels chaotic, focus on the things that you can control. Shift your mindset from what you can't control to what you can. This small change in perspective helps you feel empowered and less overwhelmed.

3. Self-Doubt and Negative Thoughts: How to Overcome Internal Resistance

Self-doubt is one of the biggest challenges to staying motivated. Negative thoughts like "I'm not good enough" or "I'll never be successful" can drain your energy and stop you from taking action.

Strategies to Combat Self-Doubt:

- Challenge Negative Thoughts: When negative thoughts arise, challenge them. Ask yourself, "Is this thought really true? What evidence do I have to support this belief?" Often, self-doubt is based on inaccurate or exaggerated thoughts. Replacing these thoughts with more rational or positive ones can boost your confidence.
- Focus on Progress, Not Perfection: A major cause of self-doubt is the fear of not being perfect. Remember, no one is perfect. Instead of focusing on the end result, focus on the progress you've made so far. Celebrate small wins and acknowledge that growth takes time.
- Affirmations: Use positive affirmations to counteract negative thinking. Repeat phrases like "I am capable," "I am making progress," or "I am resilient" to reprogram your mindset. Speaking these affirmations aloud or writing them down daily can reinforce positive beliefs.
- Visualization: Visualize your success regularly. Picture yourself achieving your goal, and imagine the feelings of pride and accomplishment that will come with it. This positive imagery can combat negative thoughts and remind you of why you're working toward your goal.

4. Lack of Immediate Results: Staying Motivated When Progress Feels Slow

One of the toughest challenges is when you don't see immediate results despite your hard work. It's easy to lose motivation when things aren't happening as quickly as you hoped.

Strategies for Staying Motivated When Results Are Slow:

- Track Your Progress: Sometimes, we forget how far we've come because we're too focused on how far we have to go. Keep a record of your progress (e.g., a journal or a progress chart) so you can see tangible evidence of your growth. This will help you stay motivated even when results seem slow.
- Set Short-Term Milestones: Break your larger goal into smaller, achievable milestones. Celebrate each milestone to maintain motivation and remind yourself that you're making progress, even if it feels slow. This creates small wins that keep the momentum going.
- Trust the Process: Understand that meaningful results take time. Consistency over time is what leads to success. Trust in the process, and remember that all the small actions you're taking are compounding toward your bigger goal. It might take a while for the effects to show, but they will eventually.

5. External Challenges (e.g., Financial, Family Issues): How to Stay Motivated When Life Gets in the Way

External challenges such as financial stress, family responsibilities, or other life issues can derail your focus and motivation.

Strategies for Overcoming External Challenges:

- Adjust Your Timeline: Life happens. It's okay to adjust your goals or the timeline for achieving them. Be flexible and realistic about what you can accomplish in the face of external challenges. A temporary setback doesn't mean failure; it just means that you may need to recalibrate.
- Seek Support: Don't be afraid to ask for help. Whether it's emotional support, financial advice, or practical assistance, reaching out to others can lighten your load and help you stay focused. This could be a friend, family member, mentor, or professional advisor.
- Focus on What You Can Control: Even when external circumstances are difficult, you can still control your attitude and your efforts. Focus on the actions you can take today, no matter how small. The more you focus on what you can control, the more empowered you will feel.
- Create a Contingency Plan: If external factors threaten to derail your progress, develop a contingency plan. Identify backup strategies or alternative paths to help you stay on track. Knowing you have a plan for setbacks can help you stay calm and focused.

6. Procrastination: How to Push Past the Urge to Delay

Procrastination is often a symptom of fear, perfectionism, or lack of clarity. It can prevent you from taking action, even when you know you need to.

Strategies to Overcome Procrastination:

- The "Two-Minute Rule": If a task seems overwhelming, commit to doing it for just two minutes. This rule works similarly to the "5-Minute Rule" and helps you break the inertia of procrastination. Once you begin, you may find that the task is easier to continue.

- Remove Distractions: Identify the common distractions that lead to procrastination, such as social media, emails, or other unrelated tasks. Try to eliminate or reduce these distractions when you're working on your goal. You can use apps or tools to block distractions during your dedicated work time.
- Create a Productive Environment: Set up an environment conducive to focus and productivity. This could mean tidying up your workspace, using noise-cancelling headphones, or finding a quiet space. A clean, organized environment can signal your brain that it's time to work.

CONCLUSION: OVERCOMING SETBACKS AND STAYING MOTIVATED

Setbacks are a normal part of any journey, and how you respond to them can make all the difference. By using these strategies, you'll be better equipped to stay motivated, push past obstacles, and keep progressing toward your goals. Remember, the road to success isn't linear—there will be ups and downs, but with persistence, resilience, and the right tools, you will continue moving forward.

CHAPTER 6: BUILDING HABITS FOR LONG-TERM MOTIVATION

Building long-lasting habits is essential for maintaining motivation over the long term. While inspiration and willpower can help you get started, it's consistent, sustainable habits that will keep you going. This chapter will explore how to create and maintain habits that support your goals, fostering enduring motivation.

THE IMPORTANCE OF HABITS IN MOTIVATION

Habits are the automatic behaviors you engage in without much thought, and they can work for or against you depending on their nature. Positive, goal-aligned habits act as the foundation for long-term motivation, while negative habits can drain your energy and lead to stagnation.

Instead of relying on bursts of motivation to push through sporadic efforts, habits allow you to make steady, manageable progress. Once a habit is established, it requires less conscious effort, freeing up your mental energy for other tasks, and becomes a natural part of your daily routine.

HOW TO BUILD LASTING HABITS

Building a habit is not an overnight process. It takes consistent effort, self-awareness, and patience. Here's a step-by-step guide to help you build habits that fuel long-term motivation:

1. Start Small: The Power of Micro-Habits

A common mistake is trying to change too much at once, leading to burnout. To build sustainable habits, start small.

How to Get Started:

- Identify a Habit: Choose one small habit that aligns with your goals. For example, if your goal is to write a book, your habit might be writing for 10 minutes every day.
- Break it Down: Don't aim to write a chapter per day—start with a modest goal like writing a paragraph or a page. Micro-habits are easier to stick with because they don't feel overwhelming.

Example: If you want to improve your fitness, don't commit to an hour-long workout every day. Start with 5-10 minutes of stretching or light exercise, gradually increasing as the habit solidifies.

Why it Works: Starting small makes the habit easy to integrate into your routine, and over time, as you master it, you can scale up. Small wins build momentum and create a sense of accomplishment that propels you forward.

2. Use Triggers and Cues to Make Your Habit Stick

One of the best ways to ensure a new habit sticks is to pair it with an existing habit. This is called habit stacking. By using an existing behavior as a trigger for your new habit, you make it easier to remember and execute consistently.

How to Use Habit Stacking:

- Step 1: Identify an existing habit you already do consistently. This could be something as simple as brushing your teeth, having your morning coffee, or finishing lunch.
- Step 2: Link your new habit to this action. For example, after you finish your morning coffee (existing habit), you could write 200 words (new habit).

Example: If you're working on building a reading habit, you could decide that every time you finish lunch, you will read for 10 minutes. The act of eating lunch becomes the cue to start reading.

Why it Works: Habit stacking takes advantage of an already established routine. When you pair your new habit with something familiar, it's easier to remember and integrate into your day-to-day life.

3. Be Consistent, Not Perfect

Perfectionism can be a barrier to habit formation. Instead

of focusing on doing it perfectly, focus on being consistent. It's more important to stick to the habit every day, even if it's in small increments, than to try and do it perfectly every time.

How to Stay Consistent:

- Set Realistic Expectations: Understand that there will be days when you don't have the energy or motivation to complete the task to perfection. However, the key is showing up and doing it even if it's not perfect. The consistency is what matters.
- Forgive Yourself: If you miss a day or struggle with your habit, don't give up. Allow yourself to make mistakes and keep moving forward. Missing one day doesn't mean you've failed—it just means you need to reset and continue.

Example: If your goal is to journal every morning but you miss a day, don't feel discouraged. Instead, get back to it the next day and continue building the habit. Perfection isn't the goal—progress is.

Why it Works: Focusing on consistency rather than perfection allows you to continue building your habit without getting discouraged. Over time, even small, consistent actions add up to significant results.

4. Use the 21-Day Rule to Form New Habits

There's a popular belief that it takes 21 days to form a new habit. While the actual time may vary from person to person, using this framework can help create the focus and commitment needed to make a habit stick.

How to Use the 21-Day Rule:

- Set a 21-Day Challenge: Commit to your new habit for 21 consecutive days. Make it a non-negotiable part of your routine for this period. Track your progress with a journal or a calendar.
- Stay Accountable: Share your 21-day challenge with a friend or accountability partner. This extra layer of accountability will help you stay committed, and knowing you have someone checking in on you increases your chances of success.

Example: If you want to develop the habit of exercising, commit to working out for 21 consecutive days. By the end of the 21 days, the routine will feel more natural, and the habit will have a much stronger foothold in your life.

Why it Works: The 21-day rule is a powerful mental framework that helps you see habit formation as a short-term challenge, making it easier to commit to. By focusing on the short-term goal, you'll find it easier to build long-term habits.

5. Track Your Progress and Celebrate Small Wins

Tracking your progress is an essential part of building lasting habits. Not only does it show you how far you've come, but it also reinforces positive behaviors.

How to Track and Celebrate Progress:

- Use a Habit Tracker: Keep a daily record of your habit. Whether it's on paper, an app, or a spreadsheet, tracking your habit provides a sense of accomplishment each time you mark it off.
- Reward Yourself for Milestones: Celebrate small victories to stay motivated. Whether it's a week of consistency, completing a certain number of workouts, or hitting a writing target, reward yourself for staying

on track. The reward doesn't have to be big—a treat, a break, or a fun activity can be enough to reinforce your commitment.

Example: If your goal is to meditate for 10 minutes each day, use a simple habit tracker where you mark off each day that you successfully complete the meditation. After 30 days, treat yourself to something meaningful, like a new book or a day off.

Why it Works: Tracking progress creates a sense of accomplishment and encourages you to keep going. Celebrating small wins helps reinforce your commitment and builds momentum to continue.

6. Make It Enjoyable

Habits are more likely to stick when they are enjoyable. If the habit you're trying to build feels like a chore, you're less likely to stick with it.

How to Make Habits Enjoyable:

- Incorporate Fun: Find ways to make the process more enjoyable. For example, if you want to develop a habit of reading but find it hard to get into, choose books that excite you. If you're working on fitness, listen to your favorite music or podcasts during your workouts.
- Create a Positive Environment: Surround yourself with people and things that encourage your new habit. Whether it's a workout buddy or a clean, organized workspace, your environment can significantly impact your ability to stick to your habits.

Example: If your habit is to exercise regularly, try doing activities you genuinely enjoy (dancing, hiking, swimming, etc.), or find a workout buddy. The more fun the activity, the more likely you are to keep it up.

Why it Works: When habits are tied to positive emotions, they feel less like work and more like an enjoyable part of your day. Enjoyment keeps you motivated, even when the initial excitement wanes.

CONCLUSION: LONG-TERM MOTIVATION THROUGH HABIT

Building habits is the key to maintaining motivation over time. By starting small, staying consistent, tracking your progress, and making the process enjoyable, you can create a strong foundation for lasting success. Habits are the tools that take your motivation from a temporary spark to a steady flame, propelling you toward your goals day after day.

Remember, motivation ebbs and flows, but with the right habits, you'll be able to stay on course even when motivation dips. Focus on the process, and over time, you'll see the lasting changes you've been working toward.

1. Habit-Tracking Tools

Tracking your progress is a powerful way to stay accountable and see your growth. Whether you prefer digital apps or physical trackers, here are some tools to help you stay on track:

Digital Habit-Tracking Apps

- Habitica: This app turns habit-building into a game. You can create your own goals (like reading, exercising, or meditating), and every time you complete a habit, you earn points and rewards. It's a great way to make habit-building fun and engaging.

- Streaks: This app helps you build positive habits by tracking your streaks. It encourages you to maintain a habit every day, and the longer you go without breaking the streak, the more motivation you gain to keep going.
- Way of Life: This app helps you track whether you complete a habit every day. It has simple yes/no checkboxes, making it easy to track progress. You can also visualize your consistency with graphs and charts.
- Done: Done is a sleek app that allows you to track daily habits and set long-term goals. It sends reminders and tracks streaks, helping you stay motivated by visualizing your consistency.

Why it Works:

- Visual progress makes the habit-building process more rewarding.
- Seeing your streaks grow encourages you to keep going.
- Habit-tracking apps help you stay consistent and motivated by making your goals measurable.

Physical Habit-Tracking Tools

- Bullet Journaling: A bullet journal can be an excellent, creative way to track habits. You can use a simple habit tracker layout (a table with dates and habits) or make it more artistic with drawings, colors, or stickers. Bullet journaling lets you track habits while staying creative and personalizing your experience.
- Habit Tracker Printable Sheets: If you prefer something simple, you can use printable habit trackers.

These can be found online for free and often come with grids where you mark off each day you complete a habit.

Why it Works:

- Physical habit trackers create a sense of ownership and help you stay engaged with the process.
- It can be satisfying to mark off a completed habit, especially when you're using colored pens or stickers.
- Journals and printables offer flexibility, allowing you to design a habit tracker that works best for you.

2. The "Two-Minute Rule" (Tiny Habits Method)

One of the most effective strategies for building habits is to start with something so small that it takes less than two minutes. This method is rooted in the idea that the hardest part of a habit is getting started.

How to Apply the Two-Minute Rule:

- Identify the Habit: For example, if you want to exercise more, commit to just two minutes of physical activity each day, whether it's stretching, walking, or doing a few bodyweight exercises.
- Scale Up Gradually: Once you start, you might find that you're naturally inclined to continue after the two minutes are up. Over time, you can gradually increase the amount of time you dedicate to the habit, but the key is starting small and easy.

Why it Works:

- Reduces Resistance: When a habit feels too easy,

there's no mental resistance to get started.

- Consistency Over Intensity: The key is showing up every day. Even if it's only for a short time, you are building the muscle memory for the habit.
- Habit Stacking: Pairing the two-minute habit with an existing habit (like doing a short exercise routine after brushing your teeth) is a powerful way to reinforce the new behavior.

3. Habit Stacking: Pairing New Habits with Existing Routines

Habit stacking is an effective strategy to make your new habits easier to remember and more automatic by linking them with already-established habits.

How to Habit Stack:

- Find Your Anchor Habit: Start by identifying a behavior you already do daily without fail. It could be brushing your teeth, having a cup of coffee, or putting on your shoes.
- Stack the New Habit: After you complete the anchor habit, immediately follow it with the new habit. For example, after brushing your teeth (anchor habit), you might spend two minutes journaling (new habit).

Example:

- Anchor Habit: Drinking your morning coffee.
- Stacked Habit: Meditate for 5 minutes.

Why it Works:

- Leverages Existing Habits: You already do the anchor

habit automatically, so adding something new afterward reduces friction.

- Easy to Remember: The action is tied to something you already do, so it doesn't require extra brainpower to remember.
- Built-In Reminders: The completion of your anchor habit acts as a reminder to perform the new habit.

4. Accountability Systems

Accountability can make a huge difference in habit-building because it adds a layer of responsibility beyond just your own motivation. Having someone else check in on you can help you stay consistent and keep pushing through on tough days.

How to Build an Accountability System:

- Find a Buddy: Partner with someone who shares similar goals or who simply wants to support you. This could be a friend, family member, or colleague. You could agree to check in regularly and share your progress with each other.
- Join a Habit-Building Group: Online communities, support groups, or habit-building groups (such as Facebook groups, Reddit communities, or accountability apps) can provide a strong support system. Share your progress and challenges with others who are also working on their habits.
- Use Social Media or Blogging: If you're comfortable, share your progress publicly on social media or start a blog. Publicly committing to a habit can increase your sense of responsibility and make you feel accountable

to your audience.

Why it Works:

- External Motivation: The knowledge that someone is expecting an update or checking on your progress can increase motivation.
- Social Support: Having a partner or community provides encouragement, advice, and inspiration when you're struggling.
- Friendly Competition: Competing with others to achieve certain milestones can foster a sense of friendly rivalry and increase your drive.

5. The Power of Rewards and Positive Reinforcement

Incentives and rewards can be a great way to motivate yourself to stick to a habit, especially when you're just starting out. The key is to find rewards that are meaningful and support your progress rather than hindering it.

How to Use Rewards Effectively:

- Immediate Rewards: After completing a habit, reward yourself immediately. This could be as simple as a relaxing break, a piece of your favorite snack, or a few minutes of an activity you enjoy.
- Long-Term Rewards: Set up larger rewards for completing milestones. For example, after completing a month of daily writing, reward yourself with a new book or a small treat.
- Why it Works:
- Positive Reinforcement: Associating the habit with a

reward strengthens the behavior and creates a positive feedback loop.

- Motivational Boost: A reward provides an additional boost of motivation to keep going, especially when you're building the habit in the beginning.

6. The "Don't Break the Chain" Method

This method, popularized by comedian Jerry Seinfeld, encourages you to commit to a habit every day without fail. The key idea is simple: don't break the chain of consistency.

How to Use the "Don't Break the Chain" Method:

- Create a Visual Tracker: Hang a calendar on your wall or use an app to track your habit each day.
- Mark Every Successful Day: For each day you complete your habit, mark the day with an "X" on the calendar.
- The Goal: The goal is to not break the chain of "X"s. As you go, you'll be motivated by seeing how many consecutive days you've completed your habit.

Why it Works:

- Visual Motivation: The sight of an unbroken chain becomes motivating. You don't want to break the streak, so you're more likely to keep up the habit.
- Instant Gratification: Seeing your progress every day can feel rewarding, even if the habit itself doesn't provide instant results.
- Momentum Building: The longer your chain grows, the harder it becomes to break it, thus reinforcing your

habit even more.

7. The 30-Day Challenge

A 30-day challenge is a structured, time-bound way to commit to a new habit. By setting the challenge for 30 days, you create a clear goal that feels both achievable and motivating.

How to Set Up a 30-Day Challenge:

- Choose a Habit: Decide on one habit you want to focus on for 30 days (e.g., journaling, exercising, reading, etc.).
- Set a Start Date: Mark a date to begin, and stick to it.
- Track Your Progress: Use a habit tracker or calendar to track your daily success.

Why it Works:

- Focused Commitment: 30 days is a manageable time frame, making it less intimidating.
- Increased Accountability: The "challenge" aspect adds an element of fun and social pressure, especially if you share your challenge with others.
- Habit Formation: By committing to a habit for 30 days, you increase the chances of it becoming ingrained into your daily routine.

CONCLUSION: TOOLS FOR LASTING HABIT CHANGE

Building habits is an ongoing process, but with the right

tools and strategies, you can stay on track and make lasting changes. Whether you prefer digital apps, physical trackers, or social accountability systems, the key is to choose methods that resonate with you. Don't be afraid to experiment with different tools to find what works best for your unique lifestyle and goals.

By incorporating the habit-building techniques discussed here, you'll strengthen your ability to stay motivated and consistent, turning your desired behaviors into ingrained habits that carry you toward long-term success.

1. Define the Habit You Want to Build

Start by being clear about the habit you want to create. Make sure it's specific, measurable, and realistic.

Examples:

- "I want to exercise for 30 minutes every day."
- "I want to write 500 words every day for my book."
- "I want to meditate for 10 minutes every morning."

2. Break It Down Into Smaller Steps (Start Small)

It's important to start with small, manageable actions. This prevents overwhelm and helps you build consistency.

Example:

If you want to build a habit of exercising for 30 minutes daily, you can start with 10 minutes per day and gradually increase the time.

3. Choose Your Habit-Tracking Method

Decide how you're going to track your habit. This could be a physical or digital method, or both.

Option 1: Digital Tracking

- App: Use an app like Habitica, Streaks, or Way of Life to track your habit. These apps give you reminders and show your progress visually, which can be motivating.

Option 2: Paper Tracking

- Habit Tracker Printable: You can find printable habit trackers online or create one in your bullet journal. Simply make a chart with the days of the month and check off each day you complete the habit.

- Journal or Calendar: Use a calendar where you mark the day you've completed your habit with an "X." This works well with the "Don't Break the Chain" method.

4. Choose Your Habit Trigger (Habit Stacking)

Habit stacking is a great way to pair a new habit with something you already do. This makes it easier to remember and integrate the new behavior into your routine.

Examples:

- Morning Exercise: After I brush my teeth (existing habit), I will do 10 minutes of stretching (new habit).
- Reading Habit: After I finish lunch (existing habit), I will read one chapter of a book (new habit).

5. Set a Timeframe (For Accountability)

Make your goal time-bound to stay committed. A good starting point is a 30-day challenge. This creates urgency and helps solidify the habit. At the end of 30 days, you'll have enough momentum to keep going.

6. Create a Reward System (Motivation)

Reward yourself when you achieve milestones. This reinforces the behavior and keeps you motivated.

Examples:

- Daily Rewards: After completing your habit for the day, treat yourself with a small reward, like a cup of your favorite tea, a 10-minute break, or an episode of your favorite show.
- Milestone Rewards: After completing a week of your habit, reward yourself with something bigger, such as a new book, a day out, or a fun activity.

7. Set Up Accountability

Accountability partners are a great way to ensure you stick to your habit. This could be:

- Sharing your goal with a friend and checking in with them daily or weekly.
- Joining an online community or group where people share their goals and progress.
- Social media accountability by posting updates about your habit-building journey.

8. Troubleshoot Challenges and Setbacks

Think about possible challenges that may get in the way of building your habit. Prepare yourself for setbacks and have a plan to get back on track.

Common Challenges and Solutions:

- Time Management: If time is an issue, try breaking your habit into smaller chunks (e.g., 5-minute workout sessions).
- Lack of Motivation: Remind yourself of the "why" behind your habit. What benefits does this habit bring you in the long run?
- Missed Days: Don't get discouraged if you miss a day. Get back on track the next day without guilt.

Example Plan for Building a Reading Habit

Let's put it all together into an actionable plan for building a reading habit.

1. Goal: Read for 30 minutes each day.

2. Small Step: Start with 10 minutes per day for the first week.

3. Tracking Method: Use a habit tracker app or a simple calendar to mark off each day you complete the habit.

4. Trigger: After I finish my morning coffee (habit stack), I will read for 10 minutes (new habit).

5. Timeframe: I will commit to reading daily for 30 days (30-day challenge).

6. Reward System:

   - Daily Reward: After reading for 10 minutes, enjoy a small treat (e.g., a piece of chocolate or a relaxing activity).

   - Weekly Reward: At the end of the week, if you've completed all seven days, reward yourself with a new book or a special activity.

7. Accountability: Share your goal with a friend or post your progress on social media.

8. Troubleshooting: If you miss a day, don't worry. Just pick up where you left off the next day and remind yourself of your goal.

STEPS FOR HABIT TRACKING

If you want to keep things simple, here's a basic outline of how to track your habit:

1. Create a Habit Tracker: If you're using a digital tracker, set it up with reminders to help you stay consistent. If you're using a paper tracker, draw a simple chart with 30 days (or however long your challenge is).
2. Mark Progress: Every day, mark an "X" or a checkmark to show that you completed your habit. If you miss a day, don't break the chain—just pick up again the next day.
3. Review Weekly: At the end of each week, review your progress. Celebrate your successes and make any adjustments to your routine if needed.

CHAPTER 7: OVERCOMING SETBACKS AND STAYING RESILIENT

INTRODUCTION

No matter how well we plan, setbacks are a part of life. Whether it's a missed workout, a skipped meditation session, or an unexpected challenge that throws us off track, setbacks can feel discouraging. But overcoming setbacks and remaining resilient is key to building long-lasting motivation. Resilience doesn't mean avoiding setbacks; it means bouncing back stronger from them.

In this chapter, we'll explore strategies to handle setbacks with grace, learn how to reframe challenges, and embrace failure as part of the journey. By developing resilience, we can continue moving forward, no matter what obstacles arise.

1. Reframe Setbacks as Learning Opportunities

One of the most powerful shifts you can make when facing a setback is to reframe it as a learning opportunity rather than a failure.

Why it Works:

- Growth Mindset: Viewing setbacks as part of the process encourages a growth mindset. Instead of thinking "I failed," you think "What can I learn from this?"
- Self-compassion: You stop being so hard on yourself and start treating yourself with the same kindness and understanding you would show a friend facing a challenge.

Action Steps:

- Ask Reflective Questions: When a setback occurs, ask yourself:
    - What happened?
    - Why did this setback occur?
    - What can I do differently next time to avoid this or handle it better?
- Journal Your Experience: Write down what happened, how you felt, and what you learned. This will help you process the setback and come out stronger on the other side.

2. Keep Your "Why" in Focus

A strong why is what drives you when challenges arise. When you face a setback, reconnecting with your deeper reasons for starting can help reignite your motivation.

Why it Works:

- Purpose-driven Motivation: When you know why you're doing something, it's easier to persevere through difficult times.
- Emotional Anchor: Your "why" serves as an emotional anchor during moments of doubt, guiding you back to your purpose.

Action Steps:

- Visualize Your "Why": Create a vision board or write a mission statement for your goal. Keep this somewhere visible to remind yourself of your purpose.
- Use Affirmations: Write positive affirmations connected to your "why." For example, if your goal is fitness, affirm: "I am committed to my health and well-being."
- Reconnect During Setbacks: When facing a challenge, pause and ask yourself, "Why is this goal important to me?" Let that answer guide you.

3. Practice Self-Compassion and Avoid Negative Self-Talk

Self-criticism can be a major roadblock to bouncing back from setbacks. It's easy to spiral into negative thoughts like "I'll never succeed" or "I'm just not good enough." However, being kind to yourself is essential for staying resilient.

Why it Works:

- Reduced Anxiety: Self-compassion reduces feelings of shame and guilt, allowing you to move forward instead of staying stuck in negative emotions.
- Mental Health Benefits: Studies show that practicing self-compassion can help you stay more motivated in the long run.
- Action Steps:
- Talk to Yourself Like a Friend: When you're feeling down, think about how you'd encourage a close friend who faced a setback. Use that same supportive language with yourself.
- Reframe Negative Thoughts: Replace thoughts like "I failed" with "I can learn from this and do better next time."
- Self-Care: After a setback, take a moment to care for yourself. Engage in activities that rejuvenate you, whether it's a walk, a relaxing bath, or reading something uplifting.

4. Build a Setback Plan (Preparation and Flexibility)

Resilience doesn't just come from how you respond after a setback, but also from how you prepare for them. By accepting that challenges are part of the journey, you can build a plan to handle them.

Why it Works:

- Proactive Approach: When you anticipate setbacks,

you can create strategies to navigate them rather than feeling blindsided.

- Flexibility: Life rarely goes exactly as planned, and being flexible in your approach helps you pivot when things don't go as expected.

Action Steps:

- Identify Possible Setbacks: Think about what challenges are likely to occur in your goal journey. For example, if your goal is to work out more, some possible setbacks might be illness, busy schedules, or lack of energy.
- Create Solutions Ahead of Time: Develop strategies for handling these challenges. For example:
  - If you miss a workout due to time constraints, plan a shorter workout the next day.
  - If you face stress, schedule extra time for rest or relaxation.
- Adjust Your Expectations: While it's important to stay committed to your goals, it's equally important to be realistic. Life happens, and it's okay to adjust your timeline or strategies when necessary.

5. Use the "1% Rule" to Stay Consistent

Instead of focusing on perfection or massive progress, aim for small, incremental improvements. This "1% rule" can help you make steady progress, even when you're facing setbacks.

Why it Works:

- Small Wins: Progress, no matter how small, adds up over time. By focusing on small wins, you build momentum and confidence.
- Reduced Pressure: This approach helps you avoid burnout or feeling like every setback is catastrophic. It's a reminder that every step counts.

Action Steps:

- Celebrate Micro Wins: Focus on achieving small, daily progress instead of expecting immediate, dramatic results. For example, if your goal is to write a book, celebrate completing 100 words today, even if it's less than your target.
- Recommit Every Day: Even on days when you don't feel like making progress, remind yourself that just doing a little is enough. As long as you're improving by 1% each day, you're moving forward.

6. Lean Into Your Support System

Having a strong support system can help you stay resilient during tough times. Whether it's family, friends, mentors, or accountability partners, surrounding yourself with positive, encouraging people makes a huge difference in how you handle setbacks.

Why it Works:

- Encouragement: A support system provides the emotional support you need when things get tough. They can remind you of your strengths and keep you motivated.
- Objective Feedback: Sometimes, it's hard to see the bigger picture when you're caught in a setback. A

trusted friend or mentor can help you reframe the situation and offer solutions.

Action Steps:

- Share Your Struggles: Don't be afraid to talk to someone you trust about your challenges. Sharing your setbacks can lighten the emotional load and open up new perspectives.
- Ask for Encouragement: Reach out to your support system for a boost of motivation or advice when you feel stuck.
- Join an Accountability Group: Surround yourself with others who are working toward similar goals. Having people check in with you regularly can provide additional motivation to stay on track.

7. Practice Patience and Trust the Process

Finally, remember that resilience is about trusting the process. Building lasting habits or achieving big goals takes time, and setbacks are simply bumps in the road. Trust that, as long as you keep moving forward, you are making progress.

Why it Works:

- Patience: Cultivating patience with yourself helps reduce frustration when things don't go as planned.
- Long-Term Perspective: Instead of focusing on immediate results, trust that your consistent efforts will pay off over time.

Action Steps:

- Remind Yourself of Progress: Look back at how far you've come. Even if you've had a setback, acknowledge how much progress you've made overall.

- Take it One Day at a Time: Break down your long-term goal into small, manageable actions, and focus on what you can control today.
- Let Go of Perfection: Understand that perfection is not the goal. Focus on consistent effort, and the results will follow.

CONCLUSION

Setbacks are inevitable, but they don't have to stop your progress. By reframing setbacks as learning opportunities, focusing on your "why," practicing self-compassion, and building resilience through proactive strategies, you can continue moving forward with confidence. Remember, it's not about avoiding challenges, but about how you respond to them. Keep pushing, stay adaptable, and trust the journey.

ADDITIONAL TOOLS FOR STAYING RESILIENT DURING TOUGH TIMES

When tough times strike, resilience can make all the difference between staying stuck or bouncing back stronger. Here are some effective tools to help you stay resilient and maintain your motivation during those challenging periods:

1. Mindfulness and Meditation Practices

Why it Works:

- Calm the Mind: Mindfulness and meditation can help calm the mind during stressful times. They teach you how to stay in the present moment rather than spiraling into worry or regret.
- Stress Reduction: Studies show that mindfulness

reduces stress, anxiety, and emotional reactivity, which are key barriers to resilience.

Action Steps:

- Deep Breathing: Practice deep breathing exercises when feeling overwhelmed. A simple one is the "4-7-8" method:
  1. Inhale through your nose for 4 seconds.
  2. Hold your breath for 7 seconds.
  3. Exhale through your mouth for 8 seconds.
- Daily Meditation: Spend 5-10 minutes each day practicing mindfulness meditation. Apps like Headspace or Calm offer guided sessions tailored for stress relief and building resilience.
- Body Scan: A body scan meditation helps you reconnect with your body and release physical tension, which can help calm your mind.

2. Reframing Thoughts (Cognitive Restructuring)

Why it Works:

- Positive Reframing: Reframing involves changing the way you view and interpret setbacks. By shifting your perspective, you can reduce the emotional impact of challenges.
- Empowerment: Reframing helps you feel more in control and empowered, as it enables you to choose a more productive and positive way of thinking.

Action Steps:

- Challenge Negative Thoughts: When you encounter a setback, challenge your automatic negative thoughts by asking:

- "Is this really true?"
- "What evidence do I have that suggests this setback is permanent?"
- "What is something positive I can learn from this situation?"

- Find the Silver Lining: Look for any positive outcomes, even if small. For example, a missed deadline could give you the opportunity to reassess your approach or refine your work further.

3. Visualization for Resilience

Why it Works:

- Positive Imagery: Visualization is a powerful tool that athletes and successful individuals often use to overcome obstacles. Visualizing success can help you reframe setbacks as temporary and motivate you to keep going.
- Confidence Boost: When you see yourself overcoming challenges in your mind, you build the confidence that you can do it in real life.

Action Steps:

- Visualize Overcoming Setbacks: When you're facing a challenge, close your eyes and vividly imagine yourself navigating through the obstacle successfully. Picture yourself feeling strong, confident, and victorious.
- Future Self Visualization: Picture your future self who has successfully achieved your goal. Imagine how it feels, what you're doing, and how your life is different. This can keep you motivated during tough times.

4. Build Emotional Agility

Why it Works:

- Emotional Regulation: Emotional agility is the ability to accept and manage your emotions without being overwhelmed by them. It's a key skill for resilience, as it allows you to acknowledge feelings of frustration, disappointment, or sadness while still making progress.
- Flexibility: It encourages you to pivot when things don't go as planned, adjusting your approach without giving up on your goals.

Action Steps:

- Acknowledge Your Emotions: Instead of pushing emotions away, allow yourself to feel them. Acknowledging that it's okay to feel frustrated, sad, or anxious is the first step toward emotional agility.
- Label Your Emotions: Name the emotion you're feeling (e.g., "I feel disappointed because I missed my deadline"). This act of naming the emotion helps you gain control over it.
- Refocus on Values: In moments of frustration, ask yourself, "What core values or long-term goals am I trying to stay true to right now?" This brings clarity and helps you reorient your focus.

5. The Power of Gratitude

Why it Works:

- Shift Focus: Practicing gratitude shifts your focus from what's going wrong to what's going right. This mindset helps reduce feelings of helplessness and enhances resilience.

- Positive Impact on Mental Health: Regularly practicing gratitude can improve your mental health, increase happiness, and boost your resilience over time.

Action Steps:

- Gratitude Journaling: Each day, write down three things you're grateful for, no matter how small. This shifts your mindset to focus on the positives, even during tough times.
- Gratitude Walks: Go for a walk and mentally list the things you're grateful for. This physical movement can help shift your mental energy as well.

6. Develop a Routine (The Power of Consistency)

Why it Works:

- Stability: A routine provides a sense of stability during chaotic or challenging times. When everything feels uncertain, sticking to a routine helps you feel in control.
- Momentum: Consistency creates momentum, making it easier to stay on track with your goals, even during setbacks.

Action Steps:

- Create a Morning Routine: Start your day with a calming and productive ritual—whether that's journaling, exercising, reading, or meditating. This sets a positive tone for the day.

- Evening Reflection: End your day by reflecting on what went well, what you learned, and what you can improve. This helps you close the day with a sense of accomplishment.

7. Social Support and Connection

Why it Works:

- Strength in Numbers: We are social beings, and having a strong support system can help us weather difficult times. Sharing your struggles with others makes you feel less isolated and more understood.
- Emotional Boost: Supportive friends or mentors provide encouragement, advice, and empathy, which boosts resilience during setbacks.

Action Steps:

- Reach Out for Support: When you're feeling down, talk to a friend, mentor, or loved one. Let them know what you're going through and lean on them for encouragement.
- Join a Community or Group: Whether it's an online support group or a local team, surrounding yourself with others who understand your challenges can help you stay motivated and resilient.

8. Focus on What You Can Control

Why it Works:

- Sense of Empowerment: Focusing on things you can control helps you feel empowered, especially during times when much of your environment feels out of your hands.

- Reduce Stress: Letting go of things beyond your control reduces stress and helps you direct energy into productive, actionable steps.

Action Steps:

- Identify Your Circle of Control: Make a list of the things you can control and the things you can't. Focus your energy on the aspects within your control, such as your attitude, actions, and mindset.

- Take Action: Focus on small, deliberate actions you can take, and celebrate each step forward. Even when the big picture feels overwhelming, breaking things down into smaller tasks helps you maintain resilience.

9. Self-Awareness and Reflection

Why it Works:

- Clarity: Self-awareness helps you understand your emotional triggers, your strengths, and your growth areas. This clarity is essential for adapting to setbacks with resilience.
- Problem-Solving: Reflection gives you the opportunity to learn from setbacks and refine your approach moving forward.

Action Steps:

- Daily Reflection: Take a few minutes each day to reflect on your progress, what went well, and what challenges you faced. This helps you identify areas of improvement and find solutions for overcoming setbacks.

- Ask Yourself Key Questions:
  - What did I learn from this setback?
  - How did I handle it, and what would I do differently next time?
  - What small step can I take today to get back on track?

10. Take Care of Your Physical Health

Why it Works:

- Physical and Mental Resilience: Physical health and mental resilience are closely connected. Regular exercise, healthy eating, and adequate rest can increase your energy levels, improve your mood, and help you face challenges with greater mental clarity.

Action Steps:

- Exercise Regularly: Even light exercise, like walking or yoga, can improve your mood and energy levels.
- Sleep Well: Make sure to get enough sleep each night to recharge your body and mind.
- Eat Nutritious Foods: Eating a balanced diet helps regulate your mood and energy levels, which enhances your ability to cope with stress.

CONCLUSION

Building resilience is a skill that can be developed over

time. By practicing mindfulness, reframing setbacks, using visualization, and leaning on your support network, you can improve your ability to navigate tough times. Resilience isn't about avoiding hardship but about how you respond to it—by staying adaptable, learning from challenges, and taking deliberate steps forward. The more tools you have in your resilience toolkit, the better equipped you will be to stay motivated through life's ups and downs.

Here are a few common types of setbacks and specific strategies for each:

1. Procrastination and Lack of Focus

Challenge: You find yourself putting things off or struggling to maintain focus on tasks.

Strategies:

- The Pomodoro Technique: Break your tasks into 25-minute work intervals with a 5-minute break after each session. After four intervals, take a longer break. This helps reduce overwhelm and enhances focus.
- Set Micro-Goals: If the task feels too big, break it down into the smallest actionable steps. For example, instead of "write a report," set a goal like "write the introduction paragraph" to get started.
- Accountability Partner: Share your goals with a friend or colleague and check in with them regularly about your progress. This external accountability can help keep procrastination at bay.

2. Burnout and Overwhelm

Challenge: You're feeling drained, exhausted, and

overwhelmed by the demands on your time or energy.

Strategies:

- Prioritize and Delegate: Identify your most important tasks and delegate or defer less critical activities. Use the Eisenhower Matrix (Urgent vs. Important) to help prioritize effectively.
- Take Breaks: Schedule regular breaks throughout your day to recharge. A short walk, a power nap, or simply stepping away from work can restore energy and mental clarity.
- Practice Self-Compassion: Acknowledge that it's okay to rest and say no. Allow yourself time to recover and recharge without guilt.
- Revisit Your "Why": When you're feeling burnt out, reconnecting with the deeper reasons behind your goals can reinvigorate your motivation.

3. Failure or Mistakes

Challenge: You've experienced a failure or mistake, and it feels discouraging.

Strategies:

- Reframe Failure as Learning: Shift your perspective by seeing mistakes as opportunities to learn. Reflect on what went wrong, what you can improve, and how you can do better next time.
- Small Wins Approach: After a failure, focus on achieving smaller, easy wins to build momentum. For example, if a project didn't go as planned, start with a

smaller task related to the project and complete it successfully.

- Seek Feedback: Ask for constructive feedback from others. This can help you see your mistakes more clearly and offer insights for improvement.

4. Distractions and Lack of Motivation

Challenge: External distractions (like social media, noise, or other interruptions) or internal distractions (lack of interest, boredom, or lack of energy) are preventing you from staying motivated.

Strategies:

- Create a Distraction-Free Environment: If possible, set up a dedicated workspace free of distractions. Turn off notifications on your phone, and consider using apps like "Focus@Will" or "Freedom" to block distracting websites.
- Set Clear Boundaries: Let others know when you're focusing and need uninterrupted time. Setting clear work hours can help reduce distractions and boost productivity.
- Use Motivation Triggers: Create a ritual or trigger that signals it's time to focus. This could be a specific playlist, a particular workspace, or a cup of coffee. These routines can help shift your mindset into productivity mode.
- Mix It Up: If the task feels boring or repetitive, try changing your approach. Use gamification (e.g., rewarding yourself after completing a task) or break up the task into smaller chunks to keep it interesting.

5. Self-Doubt and Imposter Syndrome

Challenge: You feel like you're not good enough or that you don't deserve to succeed, which is leading to a lack of confidence.

Strategies:

- Track Your Progress: Keep a success journal where you write down every achievement, no matter how small. Over time, reviewing your accomplishments can help you see that you are progressing and have the skills necessary for success.
- Challenge Negative Beliefs: When you feel like an imposter, actively counter those thoughts with evidence of your abilities. Ask yourself, "What specific achievements have I made that demonstrate my competence?"
- Affirmations and Visualization: Use positive affirmations like "I am capable" or "I am learning and growing." Visualizing your success can also help you push through imposter feelings.
- Mentor Support: Connect with a mentor or trusted friend who can remind you of your strengths and accomplishments. External validation can be a great boost when you're struggling with self-doubt.

6. Physical or Mental Health Setbacks

Challenge: Health issues (physical or mental) are interfering with your ability to stay motivated or productive.

Strategies:

- Practice Gentle Self-Care: If you're dealing with physical or mental health challenges, be sure to prioritize rest and recovery. Focus on light activities (e.g., stretching or short walks) and mental relaxation techniques (e.g., deep breathing or meditation).
- Create an Adapted Plan: Modify your goals to align with your current health status. For instance, if you're recovering from an illness, adjust your fitness goals or work schedule so they're more manageable.
- Celebrate Small Wins: When you're struggling with health issues, any progress—no matter how small—should be celebrated. Recognizing these moments can help you stay motivated during recovery.
- Professional Support: If your health setback is particularly challenging, reach out to professionals like doctors, therapists, or coaches. They can help you develop a tailored plan for overcoming obstacles while taking care of your health.

7. Financial or Career Setbacks

Challenge: You've faced a job loss, a financial difficulty, or a career setback, and it's causing stress or uncertainty about the future.

Strategies:

- Focus on What You Can Control: Take proactive steps toward addressing the financial or career setback. This could mean updating your resume, networking, learning new skills, or creating a budget to manage finances.

- Reframe the Setback: See this as an opportunity for growth. A job loss, for example, could be the catalyst for exploring a new career path or pursuing further education.
- Create a Plan of Action: Set short-term and long-term goals to guide your recovery. Having a clear plan helps reduce feelings of overwhelm and provides a sense of direction.
- Seek Professional Guidance: If needed, consider reaching out to a financial advisor or career coach. Their expertise can help you navigate the situation with a clearer path forward.

8. Relationship Setbacks (Personal or Professional)

Challenge: Personal or professional relationship conflicts are creating emotional stress or distracting you from your goals.

Strategies:

- Open Communication: In any relationship conflict, clear and honest communication is key. Discuss your concerns calmly and listen actively to the other party's perspective.
- Set Boundaries: If a relationship is draining your energy, it may be necessary to set boundaries. Protect your emotional well-being while maintaining respect for the other person.
- Reflect on What You Can Control: You can't change others' behavior, but you can control how you react. Focus on maintaining your emotional balance and responding in a calm, thoughtful manner.

- Seek Mediation: If the conflict is too difficult to resolve alone, consider seeking a third party (such as a therapist or counselor) to mediate and help guide the resolution process.

HOW TO CHOOSE THE RIGHT STRATEGY FOR YOUR SETBACK:

- Assess the Nature of the Setback: Determine whether the setback is internal (mindset, self-doubt) or external (external events, people, challenges).
- Break Down the Challenge: Focus on the specific elements that are causing the setback. Are they emotional, physical, environmental, or relational?
- Experiment with Solutions: Try different strategies from the list above and monitor how they make you feel. The key is persistence and finding the right approach that works for you.

CHAPTER 8:
THE POWER OF POSITIVE REINFORCEMENT

Positive reinforcement is a powerful tool that can help build and maintain motivation, boost productivity, and reinforce the behaviors that will lead you to success. By consistently rewarding positive actions, you create a cycle of motivation that encourages continued effort and progress. This chapter will explore how to leverage positive reinforcement to enhance self-motivation, build good habits, and overcome obstacles.

WHAT IS POSITIVE REINFORCEMENT?

Positive reinforcement is a psychological concept that involves rewarding or reinforcing a behavior to increase the likelihood that the behavior will be repeated. In other words, when you receive a reward for doing something, you are more likely to do it again.

In the context of self-motivation, positive reinforcement means recognizing and celebrating your achievements and progress—big or small. It's about acknowledging the effort you put in and rewarding yourself for taking steps toward your goals. Over time, this reinforces a cycle of positive behavior and helps you stay on track even during challenging times.

How Positive Reinforcement Works

1. Immediate Feedback: Positive reinforcement is most effective when the reward follows the action immediately. For example, when you complete a task, taking a moment to acknowledge and reward yourself right away reinforces the behavior.

2. Consistency: For positive reinforcement to work long-term, consistency is key. When you regularly reward yourself for your progress, it creates a sense of reliability and reinforcement for your efforts.

3. Personalization: The rewards you choose should be meaningful to you. What works as a reward for one person may not work for another. Tailor your rewards to what excites or motivates you.

4. Motivation through Progress: Positive reinforcement focuses not only on the end goal but on celebrating the small steps that lead to that goal. Recognizing progress—whether big or small—boosts your self-esteem and fuels continued effort.

WHY POSITIVE REINFORCEMENT IS SO EFFECTIVE

- Increased Motivation: When we feel appreciated or rewarded for our efforts, our intrinsic motivation is heightened. This makes it easier to stay focused and determined.
- Builds Self-Efficacy: Positive reinforcement helps increase your belief in your ability to succeed. When you celebrate your small victories, you gain more confidence to take on bigger challenges.
- Helps Build Positive Habits: Consistently rewarding yourself for desired behaviors helps make them habitual. Over time, this can lead to lasting behavior changes and improved productivity.
- Reduces Negative Emotions: By focusing on positive reinforcement, you shift your mindset away from self-criticism and negative emotions. Instead of punishing yourself for failures, you learn to encourage and motivate yourself.

STRATEGIES FOR USING POSITIVE REINFORCEMENT

1. Set Up a Reward System

- Create a reward system where you give yourself incentives for completing tasks or reaching milestones. The rewards can be simple (like a cup of coffee or a short break) or more significant (such as treating yourself to something you've wanted, like a new book or a night out).
- Example: If you write 1,000 words of your book, reward yourself with a 15-minute break to watch a

favorite show or go for a walk.

2. Use Self-Acknowledgment

- Celebrate small wins by taking a moment to recognize your achievements, even if no external rewards are involved. Acknowledging your progress builds a sense of accomplishment and encourages further effort.
- Example: After completing a task, take a moment to say, "Great job! That's one step closer to my goal." This simple act of self-recognition helps boost your motivation.

3. Track Your Progress

- Keep a journal or use a tracker to document your progress. This helps you visualize how far you've come and gives you something to look back on when you need motivation.
- Example: Use a habit tracker to mark off each day you follow through on your goal. Watching the streak grow can motivate you to keep going.

4. Create "Mini Rewires"

- Implement small but consistent reinforcements along the way. Each time you hit a small goal, reward yourself. This keeps you motivated through the long process of reaching larger goals.
- Example: If your goal is to exercise daily, each time

you complete a workout, reward yourself with something that you enjoy, such as a healthy smoothie, a relaxing bath, or watching your favorite show.

5. Reward for Effort, Not Just Results

- Positive reinforcement doesn't only have to be tied to completing the final result—it can also be used to encourage effort and progress. This helps you build resilience and stay motivated, even when the end goal is far away.
- Example: If you're working toward a major project, reward yourself every time you make significant progress, like completing a research phase or finishing a chapter draft, even if the final product is still a long way off.

PRACTICAL EXERCISES TO REINFORCE POSITIVE BEHAVIOR

1. **Create a Personalized Reward System**

   - Step 1: Identify your goal(s) and break them down into smaller tasks.

   - Step 2: For each task or milestone, define a specific reward that motivates you.

   - Step 3: As you complete each task, immediately reward yourself.

   - Example: Goal = Finish writing a chapter. Reward = 30 minutes of your favorite activity (reading, watching a TV episode, etc.).

2. **Visualization and Self-Celebration**

    - Step 1: Visualize the successful completion of a task or goal.

    - Step 2: Take a few moments to mentally celebrate your success. Use positive affirmations like "I did it!" or "I'm getting closer to my goal!"

    - Step 3: Celebrate in a tangible way—by taking a break, enjoying a treat, or doing something enjoyable.

    - Example: When you finish a task, spend a few minutes celebrating the success internally by saying, "I feel great about what I accomplished!"

3. **Rewarding Your Consistency**

    - Create a consistency checklist to mark off each day you maintain your positive behavior. This could be anything from daily writing, exercising, or eating healthily.

    - At the end of each week, reward yourself with something meaningful. It could be a small gift, a meal at your favorite restaurant, or even just time for self-care.

    - Example: If you stay consistent with your goal for 7 days, reward yourself by watching a movie you've been wanting to see.

4. **Accountability and External Rewards**

    - Share your goals with a friend or family member, and ask them to hold you accountable. They can provide positive reinforcement by acknowledging your progress and celebrating with you.

- Example: If you achieve a goal, call or text your accountability partner to share your success and celebrate together.

THE SCIENCE BEHIND POSITIVE REINFORCEMENT

Positive reinforcement works by activating the brain's reward system. When you reward yourself for completing a task, you trigger the release of dopamine, a neurotransmitter associated with pleasure, motivation, and learning. This dopamine boost reinforces the behavior that led to the reward, making it more likely that you will repeat the behavior in the future.

By using positive reinforcement consistently, you train your brain to associate success and progress with pleasurable rewards. This strengthens your motivation and makes it easier to stay on track, especially during tough times when motivation tends to dwindle.

COMMON PITFALLS TO AVOID WITH POSITIVE REINFORCEMENT

While positive reinforcement can be an incredibly effective motivator, there are a few potential pitfalls to watch out for:

1. Over-rewarding: If you reward yourself too frequently or excessively for every small action, you may dilute the effect of the reward. It's important to keep the rewards proportional to the significance of the achievement.

2. Using Unhealthy Rewards: Be mindful of the rewards you choose. While food, for example, might seem like an easy reward, it may not be the best long-term strategy if it undermines your overall health goals.

3. Reinforcing Negative Behaviors: Ensure that your rewards are aligned with the behaviors you want to reinforce. For example, rewarding yourself for procrastination or avoiding work can be counterproductive.

CONCLUSION

The power of positive reinforcement lies in its ability to build a positive feedback loop that reinforces desirable behaviors. By celebrating your wins, no matter how small, you create a motivating environment that fosters continued effort and progress toward your goals. With consistent rewards, self-acknowledgment, and the right strategies in place, you can unlock the full potential of positive reinforcement and keep your motivation strong, even when challenges arise.

By using positive reinforcement effectively, you'll not only reach your goals but also cultivate a sense of satisfaction, joy, and self-belief along the way. The key is to celebrate the process as much as the outcome, and to stay consistent with recognizing and rewarding your efforts.

Incorporating positive reinforcement into your daily life can significantly boost motivation and keep you on track toward achieving your goals. The idea is to recognize and reward positive behavior or progress regularly, creating a continuous cycle of motivation. Here are some additional ideas to help you integrate positive reinforcement effectively into your everyday routine:

1. Daily Micro-Rewards

- Reward After Every Task: For each task you complete, give yourself a small reward. It doesn't need to be extravagant—just something simple that feels rewarding.
  - Example: After completing a work task, reward yourself with 10 minutes of scrolling through social media, a cup of your favorite tea, or a quick walk outside.
- Use a Reward Jar: Write down small rewards on pieces of paper and place them in a jar. After completing a task, draw a reward. This adds an element of surprise and fun.
  - Example: Rewards could include "10-minute break," "listen to a favorite song," "take a 5-minute stretch break," or "treat yourself to a piece of chocolate."

2. Visual Progress Tracking

- Habit or Task Trackers: Use a habit tracker to visualize your progress. The visual aspect can be a great motivator and help you celebrate streaks of success.
  - Example: Create a daily or weekly checklist for your goals and mark off each day you achieve something. You could use an app or a physical planner to do this.
- Progress Wall or Whiteboard: Dedicate a space on your wall or a whiteboard to track your progress. For

example, you could track your workout consistency, word count for writing, or completed tasks each day.

- Example: Write down your goal at the top of the board, then add a sticker or checkmark each time you make progress. Watching the board fill up with marks will encourage you to keep going.

3. Weekly or Monthly Milestone Celebrations

- Set Up Milestone Rewards: For larger goals, break them down into smaller milestones and reward yourself once you hit each one. You could also celebrate weekly achievements to build a routine of acknowledging progress.
  - Example: If you're writing a book, set a reward for every 5,000 words written. For a fitness goal, celebrate every milestone (e.g., 10, 25, 50 workouts completed) with a special treat or experience.
- Weekend Treats: At the end of each week, if you've met your goals, reward yourself with a larger, more enjoyable reward.
  - Example: A weekend treat could be anything from a movie night, a day trip, or indulging in a favorite meal.

4. Self-Acknowledgment Practices

- Use Affirmations and Positive Self-Talk: Each time you accomplish something, take a moment to acknowledge it with a positive affirmation. This can increase your confidence and reinforce your behavior.
  - Example: After completing a task, say to yourself,

"I did that! I am getting closer to my goal every day!"

- Gratitude Journaling: At the end of each day, take a few minutes to write down what you accomplished and what you're proud of. Focusing on your achievements, no matter how small, helps you appreciate your progress.
  - Example: "Today, I finished my work ahead of schedule, and I'm proud of that."

5. Social Reinforcement

- Accountability Buddy: Share your goals with a friend or family member and check in with them regularly. This social reinforcement can help keep you motivated and give you a sense of pride when you reach your goals.
  - Example: Text a friend after you complete a workout or after writing 500 words. Having someone to celebrate with can enhance the positive reinforcement.
- Celebrate with Others: After completing a major goal, celebrate with a group or family. Sharing your success with others makes it feel even more rewarding.
  - Example: If you complete a project or achieve a long-term goal, go out for dinner with friends or family to mark the occasion.

6. Reinforce Healthy Behaviors

- Reward Yourself for Healthy Habits: Use positive reinforcement to encourage not only productivity but also well-being. For instance, reward yourself for eating healthy, getting enough sleep, or taking care of your mental health.

  - Example: After sticking to your health goals for the week (e.g., eating nutritious meals, exercising regularly), reward yourself with a relaxing bath, a favorite hobby, or a movie night.

- Mindfulness and Relaxation: After completing a task, take time to practice mindfulness or relaxation as a reward. This can help you build a sense of peace and positive feelings around progress.

  - Example: Reward yourself with a short meditation session or a walk outside as a way to unwind and refuel.

7. Celebrate Effort, Not Just Outcomes

- Reward Effort Over Perfection: Instead of only celebrating the end result (such as completing a project or meeting a goal), recognize and reward the effort that went into it. This helps reinforce the process, not just the outcome.

  - Example: If you've put in a solid effort, even if the results aren't perfect, treat yourself to a small reward. "I worked hard today, and I deserve a break."

8. Create a "Motivation Bank"

- Deposit Rewards into Your Motivation Bank: Set up a rewards system where you "deposit" rewards into a motivation bank every time you meet a goal. You can "withdraw" these rewards when you need extra motivation to keep going.

- Example: For every milestone you hit, deposit a reward into your motivation bank (e.g., time for your favorite activity). If you're struggling with motivation, look at the "deposits" you've earned and redeem them for a boost.

9. Make Positive Reinforcement Social

- Share Your Wins on Social Media: If you're comfortable with it, share your small victories on social media. Getting positive feedback from others can reinforce your motivation and provide a sense of accomplishment.
  - Example: Post a celebratory message after achieving a milestone, and invite others to cheer you on. The social validation reinforces positive behavior.
- Create a Reward Group: Join or form a group with others who are working toward similar goals. Celebrate each other's successes and use group rewards to stay motivated.
  - Example: If you're working on fitness, join a fitness group where everyone shares their weekly wins and rewards themselves together.

10. Use Technology to Reinforce Positive Behavior

- Apps for Habit Building: Use habit-building apps (like Habitica, Streaks, or Coach.me) that track your progress and send you rewards or notifications when you hit milestones.
  - Example: These apps can send you motivating messages or fun "badges" to celebrate your success, reinforcing positive behavior.

CONCLUSION

Incorporating positive reinforcement into your daily life doesn't have to be complicated. It's about creating a system of rewards, recognition, and acknowledgment for the progress you make toward your goals. Whether you're rewarding yourself for completing tasks, tracking progress visually, or sharing your achievements with others, positive reinforcement will help you maintain motivation and consistency.

Experiment with different strategies to see which works best for you. The key is consistency and making positive reinforcement a regular part of your routine. Over time, this will help you build lasting habits, improve your self-esteem, and keep you motivated to achieve your long-term goals.

To make it most effective, it's important to tailor it to your specific goals, lifestyle, and preferences. Here's a step-by-step guide for creating a reward system and tracking plan that can keep you motivated:

Step 1: Identify Your Goals

The first step is to clarify your short-term and long-term goals. Think about what you want to accomplish and break those goals down into smaller, actionable tasks.

Examples of Goals:

- Long-term goal: Write a book (completion in 6 months).
- Short-term goals: Write 500 words every day.
- Other examples:
    - Lose 10 pounds in 3 months.
    - Finish a work project by the end of the week.

- Exercise for 30 minutes each day.

Step 2: Break Goals into Actionable Tasks

Once you've set your goals, break them into smaller tasks or milestones that are easier to track.

For example:

- Long-term goal: Write a book
    - Actionable tasks: Write 500 words every day for a month.
- Short-term goal: Finish a work project
    - Actionable tasks: Complete research by day 1, draft outline by day 2, and write the first draft by day 4.

Step 3: Create a Reward System

Now that you have your goals and tasks, it's time to establish rewards. Choose rewards that motivate you and feel satisfying after achieving a task or milestone. You can use a combination of small rewards for daily tasks and larger rewards for bigger milestones.

Daily Rewards:

For tasks you complete every day (e.g., writing 500 words, exercising, working for 1 hour), assign small rewards like:

- 10-15 minutes of screen time (watch a video, play a game, etc.)
- A small treat (favorite snack, coffee, etc.)

- A break (stretch, walk, etc.)
- A few minutes of a relaxing activity (meditation, breathing exercises)

Weekly Rewards:

For bigger tasks you complete throughout the week, give yourself more substantial rewards, like:

- A favorite meal or dessert
- A movie night or TV episode of a favorite show
- A self-care activity (e.g., a relaxing bath or spa treatment)
- A social outing with friends or family
- Buying a small item you've wanted (book, accessory, etc.)

Monthly Rewards:

For bigger milestones or completing your monthly goal, give yourself a larger reward:

- Weekend getaway or day trip
- A special gift to yourself
- A full day of relaxation (e.g., reading, watching movies, etc.)
- A hobby-related treat (e.g., new workout gear, craft supplies, etc.)

Step 4: Create a Tracking System

To stay consistent and track your progress, create a system

to monitor your tasks, milestones, and rewards.

Methods for tracking progress:

1. Daily Checklist/Planner: Keep a written checklist or planner where you can check off each task completed.

    - Example: Use a paper planner or a digital one (like Google Calendar or Todoist). Each day, mark off tasks like "500 words written" or "30-minute workout."

2. Habit Tracker: Use a habit-tracking app (like Habitica, Streaks, or a physical habit tracker) to visually track your progress. These apps often send notifications and rewards when you complete your tasks.

3. Goal Progress Journal: Keep a journal where you can write down what you accomplished each day. Write down what worked well and how you felt after achieving your tasks.

4. Visual Tracker: You can create a wall chart, whiteboard, or poster where you mark off each day you complete a task.

    - Example: Use a big calendar where you add a star or sticker every day you write 500 words or achieve a daily goal.

Step 5: Plan Rewards Based on Milestones

Define clear milestones for bigger goals so you can reward yourself when you hit them.

For example:

- Book writing goal:
  - Daily Milestone: Write 500 words per day (small reward each day, like a 10-minute break).
  - Weekly Milestone: Write 3,500 words in a week (reward yourself with a movie night).
  - Monthly Milestone: Write 20,000 words in a month (reward yourself with a weekend trip or a new book).
- Fitness goal:
  - Daily Milestone: 30-minute workout (small reward: a smoothie or snack).
  - Weekly Milestone: 5 workouts in a week (reward yourself with a favorite activity, like reading or listening to a podcast).
  - Monthly Milestone: Reach fitness goal (reward: a new workout outfit or a massage).

Step 6: Accountability and Review

Having an accountability system in place will help ensure you stick to your reward system and stay motivated. This can be done through:

1. Accountability Partner: Share your goals with a friend or family member. Check in regularly to report on your progress and celebrate wins together.
2. Social Accountability: Share your progress on social media, or within a group, to receive encouragement

and feedback.

3. Regular Check-ins: At the end of each week or month, reflect on how well you stuck to your goals, track your achievements, and reward yourself for progress. You can also reassess your goals to make sure they are still aligned with your larger purpose.

Example of a Personalized Reward and Tracking Plan:

Goal: Finish writing 30,000 words for a book in 2 months.

- Daily Task: Write 500 words per day.
- Daily Reward: A 10-minute break or a small treat after writing 500 words.
- Weekly Milestone: 3,500 words written.
- Weekly Reward: A movie night or a new book.
- Monthly Milestone: 15,000 words written.
- Monthly Reward: Treat yourself to a day trip or buy something you've wanted (like a special writing tool or notebook).
- Final Goal (2 months): Write 30,000 words.
- Final Reward: A weekend getaway or a special activity to celebrate completing the first draft of your book.

Additional Tips:

1. Stay Flexible: Life happens. Sometimes you may not hit all your milestones. Don't be too hard on yourself—adjust the rewards and goals as needed.

2. Mix it Up: Make sure you mix both small and larger rewards to keep things exciting and motivating.
3. Celebrate Progress: Even if you didn't reach the exact goal you set, still take a moment to acknowledge what you did achieve.

Option 1: Using an App for Tracking

Using an app has the advantage of portability, automatic reminders, and the ability to track progress over time. Here are a few popular apps and a guide on how to set them up for goal and habit tracking:

1. Habitica (Gamified Tracking)

Best for: Habit tracking with rewards and motivation through gamification.

- How it works: Habitica turns your tasks into a role-playing game. You earn rewards for completing tasks (like gold and experience points), and you can also join groups for accountability.
- How to Set It Up:
  - Step 1: Download the app (available for iOS, Android, and on the web).
  - Step 2: Create an account and set up your character.
  - Step 3: Add daily goals (e.g., write 500 words, work out for 30 minutes).
  - Step 4: Set up recurring tasks and milestones (e.g., weekly progress check-ins).
  - Step 5: Earn rewards when you complete your

tasks, and use the rewards to "buy" in-game items, level up, or even treat yourself in real life.

Pro tip: Use the app's "Habits" section for things like drinking enough water, and use the "Dailies" section for tasks like writing.

2. Streaks

Best for: Simple daily habit tracking.

- How it works: Streaks is a straightforward habit tracker where you set up daily tasks, and it tracks your streaks of success.
- How to Set It Up:
  - Step 1: Download Streaks (available for iOS).
  - Step 2: Create a new habit by adding a goal (e.g., write 500 words, exercise for 30 minutes).
  - Step 3: Set reminders for each habit to keep you on track.
  - Step 4: Track your streak of successful days, and aim to beat your previous record.
  - Step 5: Reward yourself when you hit major milestones (e.g., 30 days in a row, or completing 5 milestones).

Pro tip: Set up 2-3 habits that align with your goals, like a writing goal and a self-care goal, so you can track both productivity and well-being.

3. Todoist

Best for: Goal and task management with easy progress tracking.

- How it works: Todoist is a task manager where you can create tasks, set due dates, and prioritize them. You can also create projects for your bigger goals.
- How to Set It Up:
    - Step 1: Download Todoist (available on iOS, Android, and web).
    - Step 2: Create projects for each of your larger goals (e.g., "Write Book," "Health Goals").
    - Step 3: Add smaller tasks under each project (e.g., “Write 500 words,” “Exercise for 30 minutes”).
    - Step 4: Use labels and priorities to keep track of urgent tasks and milestones.
    - Step 5: Review your progress at the end of the week to see how many tasks you’ve completed and reward yourself accordingly.

Pro tip: Set up recurring tasks for habits you want to track daily (like “Write 500 words” or “Drink 8 glasses of water”).

4. HabitBull

Best for: Detailed habit tracking with charts and reminders.

- How it works: HabitBull is a robust app that helps you track habits with detailed statistics, charts, and reminders.

- How to Set It Up:
    - Step 1: Download HabitBull (available for Android and iOS).
    - Step 2: Set up your habits (e.g., exercise, write 500 words) and assign them daily or weekly.
    - Step 3: Track your progress using the app's visual charts.
    - Step 4: Set up reminders for each task to ensure consistency.
    - Step 5: Celebrate milestones with built-in reward features, and visualize your progress in graphs.

Pro tip: Use the "Streak" feature to track consistency in your habits, and use the statistics to adjust if needed.

Option 2: Using a Paper Tracker

If you prefer something more tangible, a paper tracker can be equally effective, and it gives you the freedom to design your own system. Here's how to create your own:

Materials You'll Need:

- A notebook or planner
- Stickers, markers, or highlighters (optional for making it visually appealing)
- Ruler (for drawing lines if desired)

Creating a Paper Tracker

1. Choose Your Format:

    - Daily Tracker: Create a calendar-style layout with each day of the month. Use this to track daily tasks and check them off as you go.

    - Habit Tracker Grid: Use a grid format where you list your habits (e.g., "Write 500 words," "Work out for 30 minutes") down the left side, and the days of the week across the top. Mark a check or symbol for each day you complete the task.

2. Set Up Columns:

    - Column 1: Date (write the date or day of the week).

    - Column 2: Task (e.g., "Write 500 words").

    - Column 3: Completion Status (Checkmark or a symbol for completion).

    - Column 4: Reward (Write what reward you'll get after completing this task or milestone).

3. Weekly or Monthly Review:

    - Set up a Weekly Review page where you reflect on your progress. Record achievements, any setbacks, and how you felt. Use this as motivation to adjust your goals and set new rewards.

    - At the end of the month, take a moment to review your progress and reward yourself for staying consistent.

Example of a Paper Tracker (for writing a book)

Date	**Task**	**Completion**	**Reward**

		Status	
March 1	Write 500 words	☑	15-minute break
March 2	Write 500 words	☑	Small treat
March 3	Write 500 words	☑	30-minute relaxation
March 4	Write 500 words	✕	None
March 5	Write 500 words	☑	Watch a favorite show

Creative Extras for Your Paper Tracker:

- Stickers: Use colorful stickers or stamps to mark completed tasks.
- Highlighting: Color code different goals (e.g., green for writing, blue for exercise).
- Quotes or Motivational Phrases: Include a motivational quote for each week to keep you inspired.

Final Thoughts

- Apps: Offer portability, automatic reminders, and progress tracking with visual charts.
- Paper Tracker: Great for those who love the tactile nature of writing and reflecting in a physical space. It's also more customizable.

CHAPTER 9:
CULTIVATING A GROWTH MINDSET

Introduction

A growth mindset is the belief that your abilities and intelligence can be developed through dedication, hard work, and perseverance. It stands in contrast to a fixed mindset, where people believe their abilities are static and unchangeable. Cultivating a growth mindset can dramatically affect your motivation, resilience, and overall success. It's an essential component of staying self-motivated and overcoming obstacles.

In this chapter, we'll explore what a growth mindset is, why it's so important, and how you can cultivate and reinforce it in your own life. We'll also provide practical strategies and exercises to help you shift your mindset from fixed to growth-oriented.

WHAT IS A GROWTH MINDSET?

The concept of a growth mindset comes from the work of psychologist Carol Dweck, who conducted groundbreaking research on motivation and achievement. Dweck identified that individuals who believe their abilities can improve over time are more likely to embrace challenges, learn from criticism, and persist through setbacks. This mindset helps them unlock their full potential.

In contrast, a fixed mindset leads to avoiding challenges, giving up easily, and feeling threatened by the success of others. It's rooted in the belief that intelligence and talent are inborn and cannot be developed.

Growth Mindset Characteristics:

- Embrace challenges: People with a growth mindset are more likely to take on new challenges, believing that they can improve through effort and learning.
- Learn from criticism: Constructive feedback is seen as a tool for growth, rather than a personal attack.
- Celebrate effort: Effort is valued and seen as the pathway to mastery, not something that reveals a lack of talent.
- Persistence through setbacks: Rather than giving up, individuals with a growth mindset view setbacks as opportunities for learning and improvement.

THE BENEFITS OF A GROWTH MINDSET

Adopting a growth mindset can have a profound impact on various aspects of your life:

1. Increased Motivation: When you believe that your effort leads to improvement, you are more likely to stay motivated and put in the work needed to succeed.

2. Improved Resilience: A growth mindset helps you bounce back from failures and setbacks with a renewed sense of purpose.

3. Enhanced Learning and Development: People with a growth mindset actively seek out learning opportunities, knowing that their skills can grow over time.

4. Greater Achievement: Since individuals with a growth mindset tend to put in more effort and persevere through difficulties, they often achieve higher levels of success in both personal and professional domains.

HOW TO CULTIVATE A GROWTH MINDSET

Cultivating a growth mindset requires a conscious shift in how you approach challenges, feedback, and learning. Here are some strategies to help you foster this mindset:

1. Reframe Negative Thoughts

The first step in developing a growth mindset is recognizing when you have fixed mindset thoughts and reframing them. This can be done by changing the way you talk to yourself.

- Fixed Mindset Thought: "I'm just not good at this."
- Growth Mindset Reframe: "I'm not good at this yet, but with practice, I will improve."

By changing your internal dialogue, you'll begin to believe that your abilities are not set in stone, and improvement is possible.

2. Embrace Challenges

People with a growth mindset love a good challenge. They see challenges as opportunities for growth, rather than as threats to their abilities. Begin to seek out challenges in your personal and professional life and approach them with curiosity.

- Actionable Tip: Identify one area of your life where you've been avoiding challenges (e.g., trying a new skill, applying for a challenging project at work) and commit to stepping outside your comfort zone.

3. Learn from Criticism

Feedback and criticism can be difficult to hear, but they are powerful tools for growth. A key part of a growth mindset is learning how to use criticism as constructive advice to improve.

- Actionable Tip: Next time you receive feedback, instead of becoming defensive, ask yourself: "What can I learn from this? How can I use this to improve?"

4. Celebrate Effort, Not Just Results

A growth mindset values the effort and process rather than just the outcome. Celebrate the effort you put into tasks, regardless of the final result. This encourages persistence and self-motivation.

- Actionable Tip: At the end of each day, reflect on the effort you put into your tasks. Reward yourself for the work you did, not just the outcome.

5. Adopt a "Yet" Mindset

Instead of saying "I can't do this," say "I can't do this yet." This simple addition shifts your mindset from fixed to growth-oriented.

- Actionable Tip: Whenever you encounter something difficult, add "yet" to your thoughts. For example, if you struggle with a new task, tell yourself, "I can't do this yet, but I'm learning."

6. Surround Yourself with Growth-Oriented People

The people you surround yourself with have a significant impact on your mindset. Seek out individuals who embrace challenges, encourage learning, and celebrate effort. Their attitudes will help reinforce your own growth mindset.

- Actionable Tip: Identify individuals in your circle who embody a growth mindset and spend more time with them. Consider joining a group or community where growth and improvement are prioritized.

PRACTICAL EXERCISES TO STRENGTHEN A GROWTH MINDSET

1. Growth Mindset Journal

Start keeping a daily or weekly journal where you reflect on your mindset. Write down moments when you exhibited a growth mindset, as well as times when you slipped into a fixed mindset. By doing this, you'll become more aware of your thoughts and behaviors and can begin to shift them more consciously.

Example Prompts:

- "What challenge did I embrace today, and what did I learn from it?"
- "How did I respond to feedback or criticism this week?"
- "What did I do today to improve my skills, even if I didn't see immediate results?"

2. Reframing Exercise

Write down a list of fixed mindset thoughts you've had about yourself (e.g., "I'm bad at public speaking" or "I'll never be good at math"). Then, next to each one, rewrite it with a growth mindset perspective.

Example:

- Fixed Mindset: "I can't run a marathon."
- Growth Mindset: "I can't run a marathon yet, but with training, I can improve my endurance."

3. Goal Setting with a Growth Mindset

Set a goal, and instead of focusing solely on the outcome, create an action plan that emphasizes the effort and the learning process. Break down the goal into smaller, manageable steps, and focus on each step as a chance to learn and grow.

Example Goal: Learn a new language.

- Growth Mindset Focus: "I will practice speaking for 10 minutes every day. Even if I don't become fluent immediately, I will improve my skills bit by bit."

OVERCOMING SETBACKS WITH A GROWTH MINDSET

One of the most powerful aspects of a growth mindset is resilience—the ability to bounce back from setbacks. When you experience a failure or obstacle, instead of giving up, look for the lesson in the experience.

1. View Failures as Feedback

Every failure is an opportunity to learn. Instead of feeling defeated, ask yourself, "What can I learn from this situation? What will I do differently next time?"

2. Reflect on Your Progress

When you feel discouraged, take a moment to reflect on how far you've come. Even small improvements show that growth is happening, and that can help motivate you to keep going.

3. Adjust Your Approach

If something isn't working, that doesn't mean you've failed—it just means you need to change your approach. A growth mindset is all about experimenting with new strategies and learning from the process.

CONCLUSION

Cultivating a growth mindset is a powerful tool for building long-term motivation and success. By reframing negative thoughts, embracing challenges, learning from criticism, and celebrating effort, you can foster resilience and adaptability in the face of setbacks. The more you practice a growth mindset, the more natural it will become, and the more you will achieve in both personal and professional aspects of life.

As you continue your journey, remember that growth is a continuous process, and every challenge is an opportunity to learn. Stay committed to the process, and celebrate each step along the way!

Applying a growth mindset to a specific area of your life can be transformative, whether it's in your career, personal relationships, health, or creative pursuits. To help you integrate the growth mindset effectively, let's walk through how you can apply it to different areas, using practical steps and examples.

1. Applying a Growth Mindset to Your Career

Whether you're aiming for a promotion, transitioning to a new field, or improving your professional skills, a growth mindset can help you stay motivated and resilient in the face of challenges.

Steps to Apply a Growth Mindset to Your Career:

- Embrace New Learning Opportunities: A growth

mindset thrives on learning. Seek out new skills, certifications, or projects that will stretch your abilities. Even if you're in a job you find challenging, view it as an opportunity to grow.

- Example: If you're looking to advance in your career, instead of fearing a new task or responsibility, approach it as a learning opportunity. "I may not have done this before, but I will learn from this experience and improve."

- Seek Constructive Feedback: Rather than fearing feedback, welcome it as a chance to grow. Feedback is often a great indicator of where you can improve and what areas you can develop.

  - Example: Ask for feedback from your boss or colleagues about your work and how you can improve. Reflect on that feedback and adjust accordingly.

- Celebrate Effort, Not Just Outcomes: It's easy to get caught up in results, but remember to celebrate the effort and growth that happens along the way. This keeps you motivated even when outcomes aren't immediately visible.

  - Example: After completing a challenging project, reflect on the skills you developed, even if the project didn't result in the promotion or recognition you wanted. Acknowledge the progress you've made.

- Shift Your Language: Use "yet" to shift from a fixed mindset to a growth mindset. Instead of saying "I'm not good at this," say, "I'm not good at this yet, but I'm learning."

  - Example: If you feel overwhelmed by a new software program, remind yourself: "I don't know this software yet, but I will learn and become proficient."

2. Applying a Growth Mindset to Personal Relationships

In relationships, whether with family, friends, or romantic partners, adopting a growth mindset allows you to approach challenges as opportunities to improve communication, understanding, and connection.

Steps to Apply a Growth Mindset to Personal Relationships:

- Learn from Misunderstandings: Instead of seeing conflicts or disagreements as signs of failure, view them as opportunities to understand the other person's perspective and strengthen the relationship.
  - Example: After a disagreement with a friend, rather than thinking "They don't understand me," ask, "What can I learn from this situation to communicate more clearly or better manage my emotions?"
- Develop Emotional Resilience: Relationships can bring emotional challenges, but having a growth mindset helps you build emotional resilience. If you experience disappointment or hurt in a relationship, view it as part of the process of growth rather than a setback.
  - Example: In a romantic relationship, when you face a challenge, instead of thinking, "We're not compatible," think, "This challenge is a chance

for both of us to grow and learn how to navigate difficult situations better."

- Focus on Effort Over Perfection: Relationships take work, and sometimes the results may not be immediate. A growth mindset encourages you to focus on making small, consistent efforts to improve the relationship rather than expecting perfection.
  - Example: If you want to improve your communication with a partner, don't expect instant results. Start by actively listening more, asking clarifying questions, and being more patient.

3. Applying a Growth Mindset to Health and Fitness

Whether you're working toward physical fitness, better nutrition, or emotional well-being, a growth mindset can help you push through obstacles and stay consistent.

Steps to Apply a Growth Mindset to Health and Fitness:

- View Setbacks as Temporary: Setbacks like missed workouts, poor eating habits, or low energy are part of the process. Instead of feeling discouraged, see them as an opportunity to reevaluate and learn how to do better next time.
  - Example: If you skip a week of exercise, don't think "I've failed" or "I'll never get back on track." Instead, think "I've learned that I need to plan my schedule better to stay consistent."
- Celebrate Small Wins: In fitness, progress can be slow. Whether it's an extra rep, a longer run, or a

healthier meal choice, celebrate each small improvement. This keeps you motivated and shows that effort is paying off.

  - Example: If you increase your daily step count, even by a small amount, celebrate it! Acknowledge the progress you've made, rather than focusing solely on larger goals like weight loss or muscle gain.

- Learn from Challenges: Whether it's an injury or a weight loss plateau, challenges will arise. Instead of seeing them as roadblocks, look for ways to adjust your approach or learn new strategies to overcome them.

  - Example: If you're stuck in a weight loss plateau, instead of being discouraged, research different workout routines or nutrition strategies. Think of this as an opportunity to experiment and find what works best for your body.

- Focus on the Process, Not the End Result: In health and fitness, focus on the daily habits that will lead you to your goal, rather than just the goal itself. This will help you enjoy the journey, stay consistent, and maintain motivation.

  - Example: Instead of obsessing over the number on the scale, focus on the daily habit of working out and eating nutritious foods. Recognize the value of each workout or meal as a step forward, regardless of the immediate results.

4. Applying a Growth Mindset to Creative Pursuits

Whether you're an artist, writer, musician, or any other kind of creative individual, adopting a growth mindset can significantly impact your creative process and output.

Steps to Apply a Growth Mindset to Creative Pursuits:

- Embrace the Process of Learning: Creativity often involves trial and error. If something doesn't turn out as expected, see it as part of the learning process. Each "failure" teaches you something valuable.
  - Example: As a writer, if your first draft doesn't turn out how you envisioned, don't see it as a failure. See it as the beginning of the process. Use it to refine your writing and improve for the next draft.
- Push Beyond Comfort Zones: To grow creatively, you need to step outside of what feels comfortable and try new things. This could involve experimenting with new techniques, mediums, or even collaborating with others.
  - Example: As a musician, challenge yourself to play a new genre or learn a new instrument. Even if it feels difficult at first, it will expand your creative skill set.
- Reframe Criticism as Constructive: In creative fields, criticism is inevitable. Instead of viewing it as a rejection of your talent, view it as an opportunity to grow, improve, and refine your work.
  - Example: If a painting you created is criticized, instead of thinking "I'm not a good artist," try "What can I learn from this feedback? How can I apply it to my next piece?"

5. Applying a Growth Mindset to Personal Development

In your personal development journey, adopting a growth mindset can help you view self-improvement as a lifelong process rather than a one-time achievement.

Steps to Apply a Growth Mindset to Personal Development:

- See Challenges as Opportunities for Growth: Any obstacle or challenge in your life is a chance to improve your skills, develop new abilities, and grow as a person. Whether it's emotional regulation, time management, or developing confidence, there's always room to improve.
  - Example: If you're struggling with time management, instead of feeling overwhelmed, take it as an opportunity to learn time management strategies, like prioritizing tasks or using a planner.
- Develop Self-Compassion: Growth requires patience. Be kind to yourself when you make mistakes or fall short of your expectations. Remember that progress takes time.
  - Example: If you slip back into old habits or don't make as much progress on a goal as you'd hoped, practice self-compassion. Say to yourself, "I'm human, and I will learn from this experience to move forward stronger."
- Track Progress Over Time: Reflect regularly on how far you've come. Personal growth is often slow, so acknowledging small improvements can keep you

motivated.

- Example: Keep a journal or use an app to track your progress toward personal development goals. Celebrate each milestone and remind yourself of the progress you've made.

CONCLUSION

No matter what area of your life you're focusing on, applying a growth mindset can help you build resilience, stay motivated, and approach challenges with curiosity and persistence. By embracing learning, reframing setbacks, and celebrating progress, you can foster a mindset that supports continuous growth and achievement.

CHAPTER 10: STAYING MOTIVATED IN THE LONG RUN

Introduction

Staying motivated over time is one of the biggest challenges that people face. While it's easy to feel excited and energized at the start of a new project or goal, maintaining that motivation over weeks, months, or even years requires ongoing effort, resilience, and strategies to stay focused. In this chapter, we'll explore how to stay motivated in the long run by building sustainable habits, managing setbacks, maintaining focus, and continually reconnecting with your "why."

Staying motivated isn't just about relying on bursts of energy or willpower. It's about creating a system of strategies that keep you moving forward, even when the initial excitement fades.

THE ROLE OF CONSISTENCY IN LONG-TERM MOTIVATION

Consistency is the bedrock of long-term motivation. While bursts of motivation may help you start, it's consistency that keeps you going. Developing consistent habits allows you to move forward even when you don't feel particularly motivated.

How to Build Consistency:

- Start Small, Scale Gradually: One of the best ways to build consistency is to start with small, manageable goals. Rather than attempting a massive overhaul of your habits, focus on taking small steps every day that you can maintain long-term.
    - Example: If you're working on a fitness goal, instead of committing to an hour of exercise every day right away, start with 10-15 minutes a day and gradually increase your commitment over time as it becomes a natural part of your routine.
- Create a Routine: Motivation is often linked to the routines we establish. Having a set routine takes the decision-making out of the equation and helps you stay consistent even when motivation wanes.
    - Example: Set a specific time each day for a particular task, such as reading for 20 minutes every morning or writing 500 words before lunch. This establishes a habit that doesn't rely on motivation.
- Automate Your Actions: Make the behaviors you want to maintain easy to perform. This can include

setting reminders, planning your schedule in advance, or setting up environments that encourage your desired behavior.

- Example: If you want to develop the habit of working out, lay out your gym clothes the night before so that they are ready to go in the morning.

REVISITING YOUR "WHY"

When you started your goal, you probably had a strong reason for pursuing it. Over time, however, it's easy to forget that initial motivation. Revisiting your "why" is essential to reigniting your drive and keeping you on track. A compelling and emotional reason for your goal can provide the fuel you need to continue, especially during moments of doubt.

How to Reconnect with Your "Why":

- Reflect on Your Motivation Regularly: At least once a month, revisit your goals and the reasons why you started pursuing them. Ask yourself:
    - Why did I set this goal in the first place?
    - How will my life be better when I achieve it?
    - What will it mean for my family, career, or well-being?

Writing your answers down can serve as a powerful reminder when you feel like giving up.

- Visualize the Outcome: Imagine what your life will look like once you've achieved your goal. Visualizing success can reignite your passion and help you stay focused, especially during times when motivation is lacking.

- Create a Vision Board: For some, creating a visual representation of their goals and "why" helps them stay connected to their vision. Use pictures, quotes, and reminders of why you're working toward your objectives and place them somewhere visible.

MANAGING SETBACKS AND STAYING RESILIENT

Setbacks are an inevitable part of any long-term journey. They may come in the form of failure, unexpected obstacles, or a loss of momentum. The key to staying motivated over the long run is how you respond to setbacks. Rather than viewing them as signs of failure, consider them as opportunities for learning and growth.

How to Manage Setbacks Effectively:

- Embrace Failures as Lessons: Every setback carries a lesson. Instead of focusing on the disappointment, ask yourself: "What can I learn from this?" By adopting this mindset, you can use setbacks as a stepping stone to eventual success.
    - Example: If you miss a week of workouts or fail to meet a milestone, don't see it as a failure. Instead, reflect on what went wrong and how you can adjust your approach moving forward.
- Focus on Progress, Not Perfection: Long-term motivation isn't about achieving perfection every time. Instead, focus on the incremental progress you're making, no matter how small. Celebrate the fact that you're continuing to move forward.

  - Example: If you're trying to eat healthier but have a slip-up, don't give up entirely. Focus on the positive changes you've made and get back on track with your next meal.

- Develop Resilience Habits: Resilience is the ability to recover quickly from setbacks. To build resilience, develop habits that foster mental toughness, such as practicing mindfulness, positive self-talk, and stress-management techniques.

  - Example: When facing a setback, take a moment to breathe deeply and center yourself. Remind yourself that setbacks are part of the process, and staying calm and focused will help you bounce back.

AVOIDING BURNOUT AND MAINTAINING ENERGY

Long-term motivation requires sustainable energy. Burnout occurs when we push ourselves too hard for too long without rest or recovery. To maintain motivation over the long run, it's essential to take care of your physical and emotional well-being.

How to Prevent Burnout and Keep Energy High:

- Prioritize Rest and Recovery: Make sure to schedule downtime into your routine. Whether it's a full day of rest or simply taking a break after a period of intense work, rest is essential for replenishing your energy reserves.

  - Example: If you're training for a marathon, make sure you have rest days built into your training plan. Similarly, if you're working on a large project, take breaks throughout the day to recharge.

- Engage in Enjoyable Activities: To maintain energy and enthusiasm, engage in activities that bring you joy and relaxation. Whether it's reading, spending time with loved ones, or pursuing hobbies outside of your goal, balancing your focus with fun helps you recharge.
- Set Realistic Expectations: Onc of the main causes of burnout is setting goals that are too ambitious without accounting for the necessary time and effort. Break large goals into smaller, manageable steps, and give yourself grace when you don't meet every expectation.
    - Example: If you're working on a year-long project, don't expect to be at full productivity all the time. Recognize that some periods will require more rest than others.

Tracking Your Progress

Tracking your progress over time is one of the best ways to stay motivated. When you can see the small wins along the way, it serves as a reminder of how far you've come and keeps your momentum going.

How to Track Progress:

- Set Milestones and Celebrate Achievements: Break your larger goal into smaller, achievable milestones. Celebrate each milestone, no matter how small, to reinforce your sense of accomplishment.

  - Example: If you're working on a long-term writing goal, set milestones for each chapter completed. After each milestone, reward yourself with something meaningful.

- Use Journals or Apps: Keep a daily or weekly log of your progress. Whether it's a fitness app, a productivity tool, or a simple journal, tracking your progress can help you stay on course and spot patterns of success (or areas that need improvement).

  - Example: Use a habit-tracking app like Habitica or a fitness tracker to log your workouts, meals, or other health-related goals. Seeing your consistent progress over time can be a powerful motivator.

- Reflect on Your Journey: Regularly take time to look back at where you started and how much you've achieved. This can reinvigorate your motivation and remind you of the progress you've made.

CONCLUSION

Long-term motivation is not about constant excitement—it's about building sustainable habits, keeping your "why" at the forefront, and maintaining resilience through setbacks. Consistency, emotional regulation, and tracking progress are all essential tools for staying motivated over time.

As you continue working toward your goals, remember that the journey itself is part of the reward. The process of growth, learning, and overcoming challenges will lead to profound long-term fulfillment. Keep these strategies in mind, and you'll be well on your way to staying motivated, no matter how long the journey takes.

Setting up a system for tracking your progress is a fantastic way to stay motivated, measure improvement, and ensure you're on track to reach your goals. The key is to create a system that works for you—one that fits your goals, lifestyle, and preferences. Below are some steps and tools to help you build an effective progress-tracking system.

1. Define Your Goals and Milestones

Before you can track progress, it's important to have a clear understanding of your goals and the steps needed to achieve them.

Steps:

- Define your main goal: What is the big goal you're working toward? Be specific about what success looks like. (E.g., "I want to lose 20 pounds," "I want to write a book," "I want to run a 5k.")
- Break your goal into smaller milestones: What are the smaller, measurable steps that will lead to your larger goal? Breaking the goal down into bite-sized chunks makes it easier to track progress.
    - Example: If your goal is to "lose 20 pounds," milestones could include:
        - Week 1: Lose 1 pound.
        - Month 1: Lose 4 pounds.
        - Halfway point: Lose 10 pounds.
        - End of goal: Lose 20 pounds.

2. Choose Your Tracking Tools

Next, decide how you will track your progress. There are many tools available, ranging from apps to paper systems. Choose the one that feels most comfortable and sustainable for you.

Tracking Methods:

- Paper Journal or Planner: Sometimes, writing things down physically can help reinforce the process. You can use a daily planner, journal, or a simple notebook.
    - What to include: Write down the specific task or goal you're working toward, track your actions daily/weekly, and note any changes, insights, or challenges.
- Digital Tools and Apps:
    - Habit Tracking Apps (e.g., Habitica, Streaks, or Done): These are great for tracking daily habits or small milestones. You can set reminders, visualize streaks, and receive notifications to keep you on track.
    - Goal-Tracking Apps (e.g., Trello, Asana, or Google Sheets): You can create boards, lists, and charts to break down milestones and track your progress. These apps are useful for both larger and smaller tasks.
- Spreadsheets: If you prefer to have everything organized in one place, a spreadsheet (e.g., in Google Sheets or Excel) can be a great tool. You can create a simple progress tracker with columns for your goal, milestones, actions taken, dates, and results.

- Example: Track your weight loss with columns for dates, weight, calories consumed, calories burned, and exercise completed. This allows you to spot patterns and adjust your approach.

- Fitness or Health Apps: If your goal is related to fitness or health, apps like MyFitnessPal, Fitbit, or Strava can help you track workouts, nutrition, and physical progress.

3. Establish a Tracking Routine

For your progress tracker to be effective, consistency is key. Create a routine for when you check in with your progress.

Steps for a Tracking Routine:

- Daily/Weekly Check-ins: Decide when you'll update your tracker—daily for small tasks or habits, or weekly for bigger progress checks. Set a specific time to do this so it becomes part of your routine.
    - Example: Every evening, take 5 minutes to log your actions in your planner or app. Or, every Sunday, do a weekly review of your progress for the past week and plan for the upcoming week.
- Track Action and Results: Record both the actions you took and the results. For example, if you're working on a fitness goal, you can track:
    - What workouts you completed (actions).
    - How you felt after them, if you exceeded goals, or any challenges (insights).
    - Physical results like weight, energy levels, or strength improvements (results).

- Celebrate Small Wins: Celebrate each time you hit a milestone or even make consistent progress, no matter how small. Recognizing these achievements reinforces your motivation.
  - Example: If you've exercised five days in a row, reward yourself with something small like a favorite treat or a movie night.

4. Reflect and Adjust

Tracking isn't just about keeping records; it's about learning from the process. Regular reflection helps you understand what's working, what isn't, and how you can adjust your actions to stay on course.

Reflection Steps:

- Weekly Reflection: At the end of each week, set aside time to reflect on the progress you've made. Review your actions and the results.
  - Ask yourself:
    - What went well this week?
    - What didn't go as planned?
    - What can I adjust or improve moving forward?
- Monthly Check-ins: Once a month, perform a larger review. Look at the bigger picture and evaluate your overall progress. Celebrate your wins, identify any obstacles, and determine how you want to move forward.
  - Example: After one month of working towards

your goal, review your progress. Did you hit your weight loss milestone? How can you adjust your plan to ensure you continue moving forward?

5. Stay Accountable

Accountability is an important aspect of long-term motivation. Having someone else to check in with can help you stay focused and more committed to your goals.

How to Stay Accountable:

- Find an Accountability Partner: This could be a friend, family member, or colleague who is also working on a goal or is supportive of yours. Schedule weekly or bi-weekly check-ins to discuss your progress and setbacks.
    - Example: Set up a "check-in" phone call or meeting with your accountability partner to discuss your progress. You could also share progress via social media or private messaging for ongoing support.
- Join a Community or Group: Find an online or local group with similar goals. This could be a fitness group, a productivity group, or an online challenge (e.g., reading 50 books in a year). The group can help hold you accountable and provide motivation.
    - Example: Join an online writing group to share your progress, or take part in a fitness challenge on an app like Strava or MyFitnessPal.
- Track Publicly: Sharing your progress with others, even on social media or in a public space, can increase

your commitment to staying on track.

- Example: Post your weekly progress on Instagram, a blog, or even just in a dedicated journal.

6. Adjust Goals and Milestones as Needed

Goals can change over time, and life often throws unexpected challenges your way. Be flexible in adjusting your goals or milestones as necessary, but also make sure you're not giving up too easily.

How to Adjust Goals:

- Reevaluate Your Progress: If you find you're not making as much progress as you anticipated, take a step back and reassess. Are your goals too ambitious? Are there any obstacles you can work around? Do you need to change your approach?
- Set New Milestones: If you've already hit your first milestone, don't stop tracking. Set new, realistic milestones and keep working toward them.
- Break Long-Term Goals into Shorter Phases: Long-term goals can feel daunting. Break them into 3-6 month phases to stay focused. At the end of each phase, celebrate your success and adjust your next phase accordingly.

EXAMPLE PROGRESS TRACKING SYSTEM FOR FITNESS GOAL

Let's say you're working toward the goal of running a 5k in 12 weeks. Here's how you could structure your tracking system:

1. Goal: Run a 5k in under 30 minutes by the end of 12 weeks.
2. Milestones:
   - Week 1-2: Run for 10 minutes without stopping.
   - Week 3-4: Run for 20 minutes without stopping.
   - Week 6: Run 2 miles in under 30 minutes.
   - Week 10: Run 3 miles in under 40 minutes.
   - Week 12: Complete 5k in under 30 minutes.
3. Tracking Tool: Use a fitness app like Strava or a Google Sheet to log your runs, times, distance, and any notes.
4. Reflection: Every Sunday, reflect on your runs for the week. If you had a setback, analyze it and adjust for the next week.
5. Accountability: Share weekly updates with a friend who's also working on fitness goals, or join an online running community.
6. Adjustments: If you're not hitting milestones, reassess your training and make any necessary changes, like increasing your rest days or altering your pace.

CONCLUSION

Tracking progress is essential for staying motivated in the long run. By defining your goals, breaking them into manageable milestones, and using the right tools to track your actions and results, you'll create a system that keeps you engaged, focused, and moving forward. Don't forget to reflect regularly, celebrate small wins, and stay accountable to yourself and others.

1. Define Your Larger Goal

Start by clearly stating your main writing goal. For example:

- Goal: "Write a full-length novel (or X number of pages/words) in 6 months."

2. Break the Goal into Milestones

Divide your 6-month timeline into smaller milestones. These could be based on word count, chapters completed, or specific writing tasks. Since you're using a paper journal, you can write these milestones in your journal for regular reflection.

Here's an example of how you might break down the 6 months:

Month 1-2 (Foundation and Planning)

- Milestone 1: Finalize the plot, characters, and setting.
- Milestone 2: Write 10-15 pages (or about 2,000-3,000 words) by the end of Week 4.
- Milestone 3: Complete the first chapter draft.

Month 3-4 (First Draft Phase)

- Milestone 4: Write 30-40 pages (or 5,000-7,000 words) by the end of Week 8.

- Milestone 5: Complete Chapter 3 and 4 drafts.
- Milestone 6: Reach 25% completion of the full manuscript.

Month 5 (Revision and Editing Phase)

- Milestone 7: Begin revising and editing Chapters 1-4.
- Milestone 8: Write an additional 20-30 pages (or 4,000-5,000 words).
- Milestone 9: Complete Chapter 6-7 drafts.

Month 6 (Final Editing and Finishing)

- Milestone 10: Final draft revision of the entire manuscript.
- Milestone 11: Review and polish Chapters 8-10.
- Milestone 12: Submit to a critique partner, editor, or complete final draft.

3. Set Weekly Targets

Each week, set specific writing targets. These targets can be tied to your overall milestones or can be focused on specific tasks. For example:

- Week 1: Write 500 words/day (or 3,500 words total by the end of the week).
- Week 2: Complete Chapter 1 outline and write 2,000 words.
- Week 3: Complete Chapter 1 and 2 drafts.

4. Create Your Paper Journal Tracker

In your journal, you can organize your writing tracker using the following structure:

Weekly Tracker Template (Use this for every week in your journal)

Week Number	Target for the Week	Actual Words Written	Notes (e.g., challenges, breakthroughs)	Milestone Achieved?
Week 1	Write 500 words/day	[Write word count]	[Challenges, reflections, etc.]	Yes/No
Week 2	Complete Chapter 1 outline + 2,000 words	[Write word count]	[Insights, reflections, etc.]	Yes/No
Week 3	Complete Chapter 1 and 2 drafts	[Write word count]	[Challenges, breakthroughs, etc.]	Yes/No
...	...	...	...	...

- Week Number: Track the week of the month.
- Target for the Week: What writing goal you aim to achieve.
- Actual Words Written: The actual word count or pages completed.
- Notes: Any reflections, ideas, or struggles you encountered during the week.
- Milestone Achieved?: Mark whether you've reached the milestone for the week.

5. Monthly Review Section

At the end of each month, write a brief review. Reflect on your achievements and assess what worked or didn't work. For example:

End of Month 1 Review:

- Milestones Achieved: Completed 10 pages, finished character development.
- Challenges: Struggled with writer's block on Week 2.
- Action Plan for Next Month: Focus on writing more consistently, set aside 1 hour every morning for writing.

You can also include this information for each month in your journal to track progress over time. By doing this, you'll have a clear idea of where you're excelling and where adjustments might be needed.

6. Incorporating Rewards and Motivation

To stay motivated, it's a good idea to have rewards for each milestone or month completed. For example:

- Monthly Reward: After finishing the first draft of a chapter or hitting a milestone, treat yourself to something you enjoy (a nice meal, a day off, or a favorite activity).
- Mini-Rewards: After completing a weekly goal, reward yourself with a small treat (watching a favorite TV show, having a coffee break, etc.).

7. Accountability and Reflection

- Accountability Partner: If you want additional motivation, find a writing buddy or accountability partner. This person can help check in on your progress and offer encouragement.
- Reflect on Why You're Writing: Revisit your "why" for writing. If you ever feel stuck or discouraged, remind yourself why you started. This can reignite your passion and push you to keep going.

8. Adjust and Adapt

As you progress, don't be afraid to adjust your tracker if needed. Life happens, and it's important to adapt your plan as necessary. If you're consistently hitting your weekly targets, feel free to increase your goal. If you're struggling, break your targets into smaller chunks.

In Summary:

To set up a writing tracker in your paper journal:

1. Define your main writing goal and break it down into milestones.
2. Set weekly targets that support those milestones.
3. Use your journal to track weekly progress and reflect on what worked (or didn't).
4. Celebrate achievements with rewards.
5. Review monthly to track overall progress and adjust your approach.

CONCLUSION: EMBRACING THE POWER OF SELF-MOTIVATION

Self-motivation is the driving force that propels us toward our goals, even in the face of challenges. It's the internal spark that fuels our actions and helps us push through moments of doubt and resistance. Whether you're striving for personal growth, professional success, or the completion of a creative project, the power to achieve lies within you. By harnessing the principles of self-motivation, you are taking control of your journey and shaping a future that aligns with your dreams and desires.

Remember, motivation is not a one-time feeling but a mindset that needs to be nurtured and practiced. It's built on consistent action, setting clear goals, overcoming setbacks, and rewarding progress. The tools, strategies, and exercises shared in this book are designed to help you stay focused, build lasting habits, and cultivate a resilient mindset that will carry you through any challenges that arise.

Take Action Now

There's no better time than now to start applying the principles of self-motivation in your life. Take one small step today, whether it's setting your first goal, tracking your progress, or simply committing to a new positive habit. Every moment you invest in yourself is a step closer to the fulfilling life you deserve. Your dreams are within reach—now it's time to take action and make them a reality.

"The secret of getting ahead is getting started." – Mark Twain

Start now. The journey toward your dreams begins with a single step. Stay motivated, stay consistent, and trust in your ability to achieve greatness. The power is in your hands—take it!

1. Case Studies or Success Stories

i) J.K. Rowling: From Rejection to Global Phenomenon

- Background: Before becoming one of the world's most successful authors, J.K. Rowling was a struggling single mother living on welfare in Edinburgh. She battled depression and had little financial stability. The idea for Harry Potter came to her during a train ride, but the road to success wasn't smooth.
- **Self-Motivation in Action:** Despite facing countless rejections from publishers, Rowling kept pushing forward. She believed in the power of her story and was determined to see it published. Each rejection letter only strengthened her resolve. Eventually, a small publisher, Bloomsbury, agreed to publish Harry Potter and the Philosopher's Stone—a decision that would change her life.
- **Result**: Rowling's perseverance paid off in a way she could never have imagined. The Harry Potter series became one of the best-selling book series in history, and she became a billionaire author. Her story is a testament to how self-motivation, combined with belief in one's own potential, can turn adversity into remarkable success.

- **Lesson**: Even in the face of rejection and hardship, maintaining a strong belief in your abilities and goals can lead to extraordinary achievements.

ii) Oprah Winfrey: Overcoming Personal Struggles to Become a Media Mogul

Background: Oprah Winfrey's rise to fame is a powerful example of how self-motivation can transform a life. Born into poverty and experiencing significant challenges—such as abuse and difficult family circumstances—Oprah's early years were filled with adversity.

Self-Motivation in Action: Despite a difficult childhood, Oprah worked tirelessly to improve her circumstances. She pursued a career in broadcasting, starting with local news stations, and faced many rejections along the way. However, she never lost sight of her dream to help others and create a positive impact through her platform. Her relentless self-motivation led to the creation of The Oprah Winfrey Show, which became one of the highest-rated talk shows in history.

- Result: Oprah is now one of the most influential women in the world, with a media empire, philanthropic endeavors, and millions of dollars in personal wealth. Her journey from struggling to survive to becoming a billionaire media mogul is proof that self-motivation can overcome even the toughest of circumstances.
- Lesson: Oprah's story reminds us that regardless of our background or challenges, self-belief and perseverance can help us rise above and create a life

that is fulfilling and impactful.

iii) Thomas Edison: Persistence in the Face of Failure

- Background: Thomas Edison, one of the greatest inventors in history, is known for his contributions to the development of the electric light bulb, phonograph, and motion pictures. However, his path to success was filled with setbacks. Edison faced repeated failures in his experiments, and many people doubted his ability to succeed.
- Self-Motivation in Action: Edison believed that every failure brought him one step closer to success. After thousands of unsuccessful attempts to invent the light bulb, Edison famously stated, "I have not failed. I've just found 10,000 ways that won't work." His unwavering self-motivation and persistence eventually led to groundbreaking inventions that changed the world.
- Result: Edison's inventions laid the foundation for much of modern technology. His perseverance in the face of failure and rejection is a classic example of how self-motivation and an unwillingness to give up can lead to monumental achievements.
- Lesson: Edison's journey teaches us that failure is not the opposite of success but a vital part of the process. With self-motivation, even the most daunting setbacks can be overcome.

iv) Michael Jordan: From Rejection to Basketball Legend

- Background: Michael Jordan is often considered the

greatest basketball player of all time, but his rise to greatness wasn't without its struggles. In high school, Jordan was cut from the varsity basketball team. This rejection could have shattered his confidence, but instead, it fueled his desire to succeed.

- Self-Motivation in Action: Instead of letting the setback define him, Jordan worked relentlessly to improve his skills. He spent hours each day practicing basketball, developing his physical and mental game. His focus and commitment paid off when he became a college basketball star and was eventually drafted by the Chicago Bulls.

  Result: Jordan went on to win six NBA championships, five MVP awards, and become a global icon. His journey is a prime example of how self-motivation and resilience can turn rejection into greatness.

- Lesson: Michael Jordan's story is a powerful reminder that rejection and setbacks are just opportunities to work harder and prove yourself. With the right mindset and self-motivation, you can turn challenges into triumphs.

v) **Malala Yousafzai: Courage and Motivation for Change**

- Background: Malala Yousafzai was just 15 years old when she was shot by the Taliban for advocating girls' education in Pakistan. Despite this life-threatening attack, Malala survived and became even more determined to fight for the rights of girls around the world.

- Self-Motivation in Action: After the attack, Malala

could have chosen to live in fear. Instead, she used the experience to fuel her mission of advocating for education and equality. She didn't let her personal trauma stop her; instead, it motivated her to raise her voice louder and more passionately than ever before.

- Result: Malala became the youngest-ever Nobel Peace Prize laureate and a global symbol for education and girls' rights. She continues to use her platform to inspire change and empower girls worldwide.
- Lesson: Malala's unwavering self-motivation in the face of extreme adversity shows us that even in the darkest of times, our drive to create positive change can be a source of immense power and inspiration.

vi) **6. Richard Branson: From Struggling Entrepreneur to Billionaire**

- Background: Richard Branson's entrepreneurial journey is marked by his willingness to take risks and defy conventional wisdom. In his early years, Branson struggled with dyslexia and faced many setbacks as he started various businesses. His first venture, Virgin Records, almost failed several times.
- Self-Motivation in Action: Despite numerous financial difficulties and setbacks, Branson's self-motivation and relentless drive led him to build the Virgin brand into one of the most recognized names in business. He embraced challenges as opportunities to innovate and grow. His risk-taking attitude, combined with his ability to keep going when others might have quit, proved crucial in his success.
- Result: Today, Branson's Virgin Group includes over 40 companies across various industries, and he is

worth billions of dollars. His story exemplifies how a combination of self-motivation, resilience, and a willingness to take calculated risks can lead to extraordinary success.

- Lesson: Branson's journey is a clear reminder that self-motivation, paired with a willingness to learn from mistakes and keep moving forward, can turn even the toughest challenges into success.
- Steve Jobs and Apple: Jobs' ability to stay motivated through setbacks—such as being ousted from Apple, the company he founded—demonstrates how self-belief and motivation can lead to one of the most successful comebacks in business history. His eventual return to Apple and its subsequent success is a testament to the power of resilience and self-motivation.
- The Story of Sarah Robb O'Hagan: Sarah went from being told she wasn't cut out for leadership roles to becoming the CEO of Flywheel Sports. Her story is one of overcoming self-doubt and pushing through failure. Her belief in her abilities and staying motivated through challenges were key to her success.

2. Exercises or Journal Prompts

Encouraging readers to reflect on their own motivation levels and personal challenges is an effective way to make the book more interactive. Here are some journal prompts and exercises:

Journal Prompts for Self-Reflection:

- What motivates me? Take a moment to reflect on

what truly drives you. Is it personal growth? Family? Financial freedom? Write down your top motivators.

- When have I felt most motivated in the past? Think back to a time when you felt unstoppable. What were the circumstances? What factors helped you stay focused and determined? Write about this experience.
- What are my top 3 biggest obstacles to staying motivated? Identify the barriers that hold you back from achieving your goals. These might be fear, procrastination, lack of time, etc.
- What's one small change I can make today to boost my motivation? This could be a daily habit, a new mindset, or a new action that will get you closer to your goals. Write down one simple change and commit to it.

Self-Motivation Exercise:

- Create Your Personal Vision Statement: Write a vision statement for your life, one that reflects the person you want to become and the goals you want to achieve. Be as specific as possible. For example: "I am a confident, resilient, and creative writer who consistently writes 1,000 words a day and has published my first book within the next year."
- Weekly Motivation Check-In: Every Sunday, review your progress toward your goals. How did you feel during the week? Did you hit your targets? What are the obstacles you faced, and how did you overcome them? Write your answers and make adjustments to the upcoming week's plan as needed.

3. Actionable Tips for Staying Motivated Daily

Providing small, actionable tips can help readers integrate motivation strategies into their daily lives. Here are some practical ideas:

Actionable Daily Motivation Tips:

1. Start Small: Focus on one task at a time. Don't overwhelm yourself with everything at once. Break your big goal into tiny steps and celebrate each small win.

2. Morning Routine: Start your day with a simple habit that sets the tone for the rest of the day. This could be something like journaling, stretching, or setting intentions for the day. A good morning routine boosts focus and motivation.

3. Visualize Your Success: Spend 5-10 minutes each day visualizing your success. Imagine what it would feel like to accomplish your goals. This mental practice can motivate you to stay on track.

4. Accountability Partner: Find someone to check in with regularly. Having someone to hold you accountable can be a powerful motivator. Whether it's a friend, colleague, or online community, accountability increases your chances of success.

5. Use the Two-Minute Rule: If a task feels overwhelming, break it down to something that takes only 2 minutes. Often, just starting is the hardest part, and the momentum will carry you through.

6. Track Your Progress: Use a simple habit tracker or

journal to log daily actions toward your goals. Seeing progress, even in small increments, can be incredibly motivating.

7. Reward Yourself: Implement a reward system for completing specific tasks or milestones. Whether it's a break, a treat, or an activity you enjoy, rewards keep you motivated throughout the process.
8. Focus on Your "Why": Remind yourself why you started this journey in the first place. Whenever motivation wanes, revisiting your core reasons for pursuing the goal can reignite your drive.

4. Additional Tools for Motivation

To help readers stay motivated, you can suggest additional tools and resources that can complement the strategies discussed in the book:

1. Motivational Apps: Apps like Habitica, Forest, or Streaks can help readers build habits and track their progress toward their goals. Many of these apps make the process of tracking fun by incorporating gamification.
2. Daily Affirmations: Encourage readers to write daily affirmations that align with their goals. This could be statements like: "I am focused, determined, and capable of achieving my goals," or "Every step I take brings me closer to my dreams."
3. Motivational Podcasts or Books: Suggest motivational podcasts like The Tony Robbins Podcast or The School of Greatness with Lewis

Howes. Additionally, recommend inspirational books that reinforce the ideas discussed in your book, such as Atomic Habits by James Clear or The Power of Now by Eckhart Tolle.

4. Mind Mapping: Use mind mapping tools or apps like MindMeister to visualize the path to success. Breaking down your larger goals into sub-goals visually can help keep you motivated and focused.

9789364021319